Math Works

Montessori math and the developing brain

by
Michael Duffy

Parent Child Press
PO Box 675
Hollidaysburg, PA 16648

Copyright © 2008 Michael Duffy. All rights reserved.

Cover Photographer: Frida Azari
Book Design: Shauna McDonough

Photographers:
Frida Azari pp. 1, 5, 25, 34, 35, 37, 38, 39, 40, 42, 43, 60, 61, 66, 69, 70, 71
Michael Duffy: p. 3
Wendy Shenk-Evans: pp. 8, 18

Library of Congress Control Number: 2008922638
ISBN # 0-939195-38-0

No part of this book may be used or reproduced in any manner whatsoever without written permission except in the case of brief quotations embodied in critical articles and reviews.

*This book is dedicated to
D'Neil Duffy, my wife, and my long-time partner
and inspiration in Montessori.*

Acknowledgments

I want to thank:

D'Neil Duffy, for her patience, support and constant encouragement in this project; my daughter, Mignon Duffy, PhD, who helped me find my own voice in the chapter on brain development; Catherine Maresca, my editor, for helping me to clarify my explanations of the materials in Chapter 2. And the following readers who offered many useful suggestions: Wendy Shenk-Evans, Melinda Melone, Aline Wolf.

Thanks to the students and staff at La Nueva Escuela Juan Ponce de Leon in Puerto Rico for the picture of their classroom that illustrates the beauty of a Montessori class.

I would also like to offer thanks to Wendy Shenk-Evans for her photos and a special thank you to Frida Azari for the photos that grace the cover and are spread throughout the book to

Table of Contents

Introduction..1

Chapter 1 – Developing a Mathematical Mind 3

Chapter 2 – Concrete Materials to Learn Abstract Concepts 9

Chapter 3 – The Benefits of Montessori Math Materials 34

Chapter 4 – Montessori Math and the Human Brain 46

Chapter 5 – Montessori Math, Standards and Testing 59

Chapter 6 – A Plea to Parents..65

Appendix..71

Bibliography...76

About the Author...78

Introduction

Montessori math materials are wonderful tools for your child to learn mathematics, help him[1] develop his full potential as a human being and build his brain power.

This book is addressed primarily to parents of a Montessori child. You have made a choice to entrust the education of your child to a pedagogy that is perhaps unfamiliar to you, a leap of faith that deserves some reassurance from time to time.

One area of particular concern is mathematics. The math shelves in Montessori classrooms are filled with colorful but mysterious materials that you hear your child refer to as he talks about his work in school – such as the stamp game, bead frame, checkerboard, and trinomial cube.

You probably embraced the Montessori program without reservation when you first enrolled him as a 2- or 3-year-old, but you may have gotten nervous as he moved toward the elementary level, where things like math start to "count for real."

If you are going to understand and support the Montessori program, you need to know what these materials are, what benefits they offer your child academically, psychologically and developmentally, how they affect the growth of your child's brain, and how they prepare him for a standardized math test. That is the primary purpose of this book.

---

[1] Throughout this book, I will alternate between masculine and feminine pronouns to refer to your child, changing each chapter.

The book is also intended for:
- Montessori classroom teachers, to remind them of the reasons they teach the way they do and to help them avoid the temptation of taking precious time away from the Montessori materials for textbooks and workbooks.
- Montessori administrators, to reassure them that the Montessori approach to math is giving children what they need to meet the recognized academic standards and to help them respond to concerned parents who raise questions about the Montessori materials.
- Non-Montessori educators, who may wish to know more about the Montessori math materials when receiving or working with students from Montessori programs.

The book begins with Maria Montessori's emphasis on development in the learning process, particularly the development of the "mathematical mind" in the subject area of math. Chapter 2 gives an introductory glimpse of the principal Montessori materials used to teach math at the primary and elementary levels.

Switching from the question of "What?" to the all-important correlative "So what?" Chapter 3 examines the benefits of the Montessori approach from the perspective of research done by developmental psychologists and educators. Chapter 4 uses the findings of modern brain research to evaluate what takes place in the brain of children working with the Montessori math materials. And Chapter 5 relates the Montessori math curriculum to state standards and standardized tests.

The final chapter is a plea to you as parents. I urge you to trust the Montessori math curriculum and not to pressure your child's teacher to use a lot of workbooks or assign a lot of homework to meet your needs - at the expense of your child's development and brain growth.

My appeal to you as parents comes from my experience of seeing teachers abandon good Montessori practice in the face of parental challenges. I firmly believe that you will be enthusiastic supporters of the Montessori approach to math (and education in general) as you see its benefits for your child.

Chapter 1

Developing a Mathematical Mind

What an intriguing place this Montessori classroom is!

As parents who take the time to observe in a Montessori elementary classroom, you often find yourselves in a new world, quite different from anything you may have experienced in your own education.

Children are gathered at tables or working on a rug on the floor rather than sitting quietly in rows of desks. There are students of various ages in the same classroom, forming a three-year age group of social peers. Children are working together, talking and discussing their work. Instead of using textbooks, these students are working with colorful materials taken from shelves along the walls and throughout the room.

One of the most intriguing parts of the elementary classroom is the area of the room dedicated to the math materials. This is where you will find a fairly standard collection of materials in Montessori classrooms anywhere in the world, regardless of the differences that might exist in other parts of the room.

There are boxes of beads and colorful tiles, charts of numbers, long chains of colored beads, metal pie charts, a three-color checkerboard, and even a collection of test tubes with colored beads in them. There are boxes of pie-shaped pieces, tiny colored disks that students use with a yellow board, a board that looks like it came from the local hardware store with colored pegs to put in it, boxes with puzzle pieces arranged in a cube, and sets of colored blocks that look like they belong in a kindergarten room instead of an elementary classroom.

Obviously, if you have chosen a Montessori school for your child, you probably already know something about this hands-on, concrete, materials-based approach to education and believe it's a good thing for your child. But we Montessori teachers sometimes do an incomplete job of explaining why all these materials are so beneficial for your child. And when it comes time to prepare for standardized tests and a possible move to a school with more traditional approaches to math, you might get a little nervous about all these games we play with mathematics in Montessori.

Here is some of the theory behind the materials.

Montessori is a Developmental Approach to Education

Let's start with the overall educational goals of a Montessori approach to education. The difference between a Montessori classroom and a typical classroom in a "traditional" or "conventional" setting is not just the lack of textbooks, the multi-age groupings, the collaborative approach to student work or the shelves of materials. There is something more important that is harder to observe during a casual visit to the classroom. Your child's academic progress is viewed as a welcome byproduct of the main focus of the school - the development of the whole child, not just intellectually, but also emotionally, socially, and even spiritually. This development is the fruit of the child's work.

Maria Montessori draws a distinction between the work of the adult, which is directed toward producing useful commodities, and the work of a child, directed toward producing an adult person within himself. "Although he cannot share in the work of adults, he has his own difficult and important task to perform, that of producing a man....It is solely from a child that a man is formed. An adult cannot take part in this labor...We can thus constantly repeat, 'The child is the father of the man.'"[2]

As a physician and scientist, Montessori spent her life observing how children grow and develop into adults, and she created an educational system designed to maximize that growth and development at each stage of the child's life. From the infant-toddler level through high school, this is a constant in authentic Montessori schools.

A Montessori education promotes your child's emotional health and development. Montessori wanted your child to constantly grow in independence, building his self-esteem and self-confidence so he can succeed in life as an adult. Self-esteem is a major indicator of that future success.

Social development is another priority in a Montessori classroom, and so your child is given the opportunity to interact with others all day long. He is taught how to collaborate, to resolve conflicts peacefully, to understand real friendship, to respect and care for others. In a world that values fierce competition and winning at all costs, this seems to go against the grain of society. However, it is vital for developing the child into the kind of adult who can promote world peace.

Even spiritual development is part of the Montessori program. Most Montessori schools are not religious, but there are spiritual elements of development that are important outcomes of our work with your child.[3] He is taught to value his own dignity, to respect the rights of others, to appreciate beauty and art, to recognize good choices, to serve others, and to be part of something bigger than himself. On an even deeper level, your child

---

[2] Montessori, Maria. *The Secret of Childhood*. Fides Publishers: Notre Dame, Indiana. 1966. pp. 236-237.
[3] For a thorough discussion of this element of the Montessori program, see Aline Wolf's book, *Nurturing the Spirit in Non-Sectarian Classrooms*, Parent Child Press, Hollidaysburg, PA, 1996.

becomes conscious of his unity with all other humans, with every living organism, and with the universe itself; from this he will begin to understand his "cosmic task," or contribution to the world, as a member of the human species and as an individual.[4]

Intellectual development, of course, is also one of the goals of education. However, such development is impossible - or at least extraordinarily difficult - if your child does not enjoy self-esteem, healthy relationships with others and a strong value system. If he doesn't believe he is capable or academically competent, he probably won't be. If your child is in an emotional state over a disagreement with a close friend - a common situation for elementary aged children - it is almost impossible for him to concentrate on an academic task. If he sees no value in growing and learning, he has little incentive to work at it. Academic success builds on the foundation of the other areas of development in his life.

Montessori's Ideas about Developing the Mathematical Mind

Mathematics, perhaps more than any of the other subjects, is directed to pure intellectual development - although, in a Montessori context and with the Montessori approach, it also promotes emotional, social and spiritual development as well.

The intellectual development envisioned by a Montessori education is not limited to academic achievement - or even directed primarily to that end. Most people tend to think of arithmetic, algebra and geometry, the main mathematical disciplines in an elementary program, as ways to teach children to find answers to problems as quickly and efficiently as possible. That's certainly the way most of the parents of Montessori children were taught, and it's the way children are tested in our society to see if they are making acceptable progress.

Montessori mathematics is different. The focus is not on the answer - it's on how your child gets the answer. This is contrary to the usual way we operate in the adult world, where results are the primary goal, to be reached as quickly as possible.

---

[4] For a detailed discussion of "cosmic education," see Michael and D'Neil Duffy's book, *Children of the Universe: Cosmic Education in the Montessori Elementary Classroom*, Parent Child Press, Hollidaysburg, PA 2002.

"This illustrates one of the fundamental differences between the natural laws of work for children and for adults. A child does not follow the law of minimum effort, but rather the very opposite. He consumes a great deal of energy in working for no ulterior end and employs all his potentialities in the execution of each detail. The external object and action are in every case of only accidental importance."[5]

Maria Montessori's educational focus was the "psychic development" of the child. Hence, the title of her book about her mathematics program – *Psicoaritmetica*.[6] Montessori coined this word to give the idea that she was more interested in the impact on a child's mind than on teaching pure technique. Her goal in this book was not just to offer a way for children to learn "the necessary and basic culture" of mathematics (how to get the right answers) but a way to use arithmetic as a "means for the development of the mind."[7]

In other words, the purpose of her educational program and the mathematics curriculum in particular was developmental. Specifically, the math curriculum was designed to develop the child's "mathematical mind," a phrase I will use repeatedly in this book to indicate the overall goal of the curriculum in this area. Montessori herself called the materials she developed for learning arithmetic "a gym for mental gymnastics"[8] to assist children in learning to think and reason logically and clearly.

In her preface to the original Spanish edition of the book, she expresses personal pride in the fact that in 25 years of experience no other area of curriculum so engaged the children and produced such amazing results as that of mathematics.

Mario Montessori, her son and close collaborator, in his preface to the Italian edition of *Psicoaritmetica*, emphasizes the developmental nature of his mother's approach. "The focus is not on the mastery of rules and

---

[5] Montessori, *Secret*, p. 240.
[6] Montessori, Maria. *Psicoaritmetica: L'aritmetica sviluppata secondo le indicazioni della psicologia infantile durante venticinque anni di esperienze. (Arithmetic Developed According to the Dictates of Child Psychology during Twenty-Five years of Experiences)* Garzanti, 1971. p. 2. (author's translation from the Italian edition). Originally published in Spanish in 1934.
[7] Ibid. p. 1.
[8] Ibid. p. 1.

techniques, but in promoting the understanding of that which mathematics expresses. Maria Montessori always moved in this direction: for her the central point of education is the child and his development."[9]

And so, Maria Montessori would have been dismayed at our current obsession with test scores. For her, the study of mathematics was not designed just to produce children who could get the right answers on the test. Her vision, as always, was much more ambitious. She wanted to make sure that children developed their "mathematical mind" - that they learned how to think with precision and logic.

The brain research that will be discussed later in this book had not been developed before her death, so she was unable to express her goals in terms of brain building. But, as we shall see, she anticipated those findings in a significant way with her ideas about the "mathematical mind" and her math materials.

Before we talk about building the brain, let's take a look at the design of those materials.

---

[9] Ibid. p.V.

Chapter 2
Concrete Materials to Learn Abstract Concepts

How did Maria Montessori design her curriculum and materials to promote the development of the "mathematical mind" of your child? What are all those intriguing materials you see on the shelves? And how are they used by your child?

This chapter will describe some of the key materials used in teaching your child mathematics in a Montessori context. It will not deal with every material or every presentation of those materials, but it should give you an idea of what she is exposed to in school and what she is talking about when she comes home and tells you what she learned today.[10]

One of the most basic principles of Montessori mathematics is that students always learn new concepts with concrete materials. Montessori's math materials are designed to lead your child step by step from the most concrete representation to pure abstraction.

Learning to Count

The first step in mastering mathematics is learning to count. But counting is much more than just reciting numbers in sequence - it involves matching word and written symbols to real quantities. A young child reciting the numbers 1-10 from memory and drill is no more an example of real counting than the sing-song recitation of the alphabet is the same as reading. Counting on her fingers may not have meant anything more to her than a way to name her fingers. The Montessori materials bring your child beyond that stage to a more concrete understanding of number-quantity correspondence.

---

[10] For a full list of the wealth of math materials available to your child in a typical Montessori classroom, see the appendix at the end of this book.

One of the earliest concrete materials used to teach counting are the number rods, which is one of several materials your child has at her disposal to match the numbers 1-10 to those quantities. The number rods go from a 10-centimeter length representing the number 1 to a meter-long strip of alternating red and blue lengths representing the number 10.

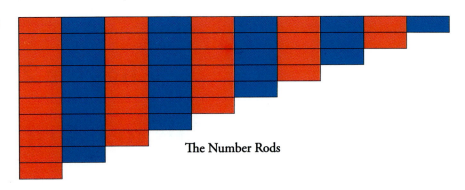

The Number Rods

Your child then works with the teen boards and ten boards to count from 1-100. She uses the long bead chains, a color-coded collection of connected bead bars, to count to 1,000.

And she learns how the decimal system works using the golden bead materials, with ten unit beads making a ten bar, 10 ten bars making a hundred square, and 10 hundred squares making a thousand cube.

Your child can hold a unit bead in one hand and a thousand cube in the other to have a sensory-based impression of the difference between them. A thousand cube is 1000 times as big as a unit bead, it's 1000 times as heavy, and it has 1000 times the value - because it actually contains 1000 unit beads. You can't get more concrete than that!

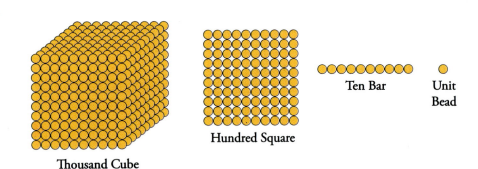

Thousand Cube   Hundred Square   Ten Bar   Unit Bead

Later, your child learns to form numbers into the millions, billions and even higher as she works with other materials. She is introduced to counting by fractions with the metal fraction insets, red and green materials that look like pie charts divided into fractions from halves to tenths. She learns to count in decimals with materials combining colored beads to represent the whole numbers and lighter shaded discs or cubes (depending on the materials manufacturer) to represent decimal fractions up to the millionths. There are special beads for her to distinguish positive and negative numbers. And she uses materials like the binomial and trinomial cubes to learn algebraic numeration.

The Four Basic Operations with Whole Numbers

At first, your child will learn to add, subtract, multiply and divide. If she can do these four operations with whole numbers, fractions and decimals, that constitutes the bulk of what she is expected to learn by the time she finishes elementary school - although, as you will see, she learns a lot more in a Montessori program.

The golden beads are among the most important materials in teaching Montessori mathematics. In addition to giving your child a concrete understanding of the decimal system, they are the first and most concrete Montessori tool for teaching her to add, subtract, multiply and divide whole numbers.

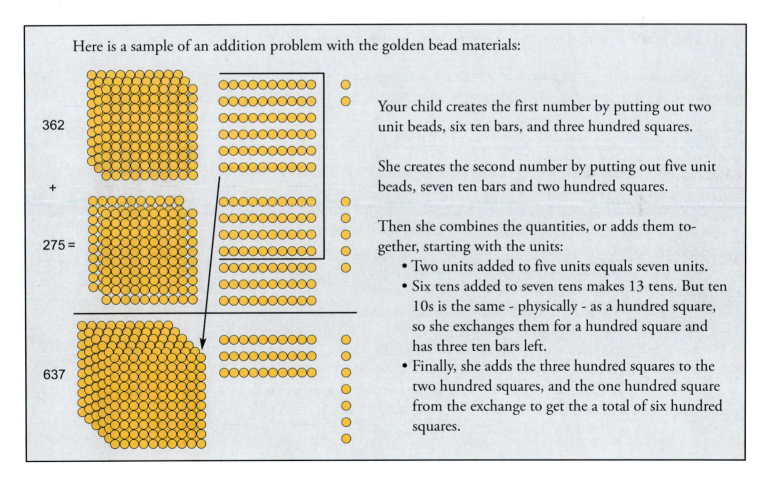

Here is a sample of an addition problem with the golden bead materials:

362
+
275 =

637

Your child creates the first number by putting out two unit beads, six ten bars, and three hundred squares.

She creates the second number by putting out five unit beads, seven ten bars and two hundred squares.

Then she combines the quantities, or adds them together, starting with the units:
- Two units added to five units equals seven units.
- Six tens added to seven tens makes 13 tens. But ten 10s is the same - physically - as a hundred square, so she exchanges them for a hundred square and has three ten bars left.
- Finally, she adds the three hundred squares to the two hundred squares, and the one hundred square from the exchange to get the a total of six hundred squares.

In addition, your child puts the two quantities together, with exchanges made whenever the combination produces a number higher than 10 (as in the above example). The process is the same whether she is adding one-digit numbers or four digit numbers.

For subtraction, your child removes the second quantity from the first. For multiplication, she does the same process as she did in addition, but all the numbers she puts together are the same. For division, she distributes the golden bead materials so each unit in the divisor gets an equal share.

The golden beads use physical quantities of beads to perform the four operations. The first step toward abstraction involves the "stamp game." This material uses squares, all the same size - a green square with a "1" on it to represent a unit bead, blue with a "10" on it to replace the 10 bar, red with a "100" on it to represent the hundred square, and back to a green square, but this time with "1000" on it, to replace the thousand cube.

These materials are a lot less bulky than the golden bead materials. More importantly, they move your child one step toward abstraction while maintaining a very concrete representation of the process of addition.

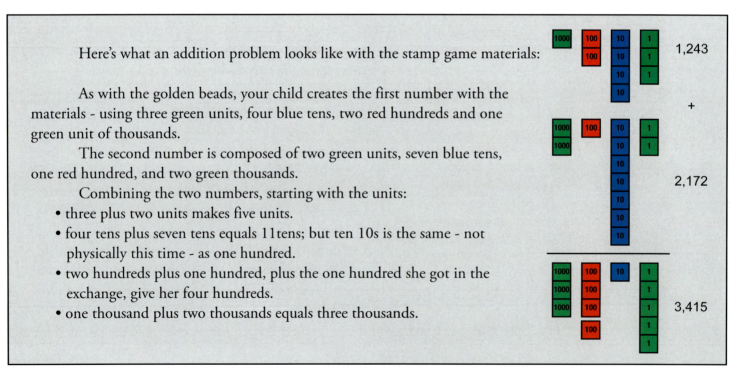

Here's what an addition problem looks like with the stamp game materials:

As with the golden beads, your child creates the first number with the materials - using three green units, four blue tens, two red hundreds and one green unit of thousands.

The second number is composed of two green units, seven blue tens, one red hundred, and two green thousands.

Combining the two numbers, starting with the units:
- three plus two units makes five units.
- four tens plus seven tens equals 11 tens; but ten 10s is the same - not physically this time - as one hundred.
- two hundreds plus one hundred, plus the one hundred she got in the exchange, give her four hundreds.
- one thousand plus two thousands equals three thousands.

The stamp game also can be used to do subtraction, multiplication and division of whole numbers. For division, special place holders called "skittles" are used to represent the units, tens and hundreds in one- two- and three-digit divisors. There is even a large green skittle to represent thousands so your child can do four-digit divisors.

Once again, for all these operations, it makes no difference whether your child is calculating with one-digit numbers or four-digit numbers. The process is the same, and it's not dependent on memorization of tables.

The small and large bead frames provide your child yet another step toward abstraction, as well as the ability to do bigger problems in addition and subtraction, and multiplication problems with multiple-digit multiplicands. Here, there are no numbers on the beads to use as guides. Only the colors remain to distinguish the units, tens, hundreds and thousands.

Here's a sample addition problem your child could do on the small bead frame:

First, she counts off four units, one ten, five hundreds and one thousand for the first addend, moving the beads from the left side of the frame to the right.

Next, she starts to add the second number, starting with the units.

- To move eight more units over to the right side, she has to make an exchange for one ten when she runs out of units, moving the ten units back to the left side in exchange for the ten she moves to the right side. Now she can move the remaining two units to the right.
- She now has her original ten from the first number and the ten from the exchange. She moves over the four tens from the second number, and she gets a total of six tens.
- She moves over three hundreds and two thousands, and neither addition requires any exchanges.

1514 + 2348 = 3862

Your child uses the small bead frame for addition, subtraction and multiplication. The large bead frame is designed like the small one, but it has three more rows of beads, which allows her to solve problems into the millions. By this time, she uses it mostly for compound multiplication, with two and three-digit multipliers.

The bead frame is accompanied by special bead frame papers which allow your child to begin making note of how numbers are broken down in a multi-digit multiplication problem (e.g. 348 x 23 = [8 + 40 + 300] x [3 + 20] = 3 [8 + 40 + 300] + 20 [8 + 40 + 300])

Another major material for learning compound multiplication is the checkerboard, which is designed for problems up to four-digit multipliers and as many as nine-digit multiplicands!

The board is accompanied by a box of colored bead bars, with different colors to represent the numbers one through nine. By placing these bead bars on the proper square of the checkerboard, they take the value of the hierarchy where they are placed.

Here is a sample of a problem with a three-digit multiplier: 5273 x 426 =

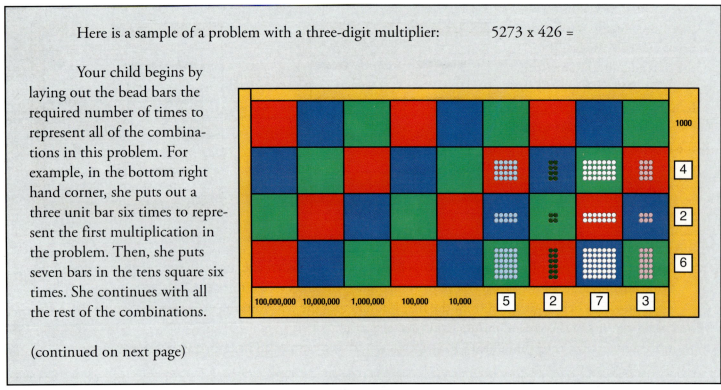

Your child begins by laying out the bead bars the required number of times to represent all of the combinations in this problem. For example, in the bottom right hand corner, she puts out a three unit bar six times to represent the first multiplication in the problem. Then, she puts seven bars in the tens square six times. She continues with all the rest of the combinations.

(continued on next page)

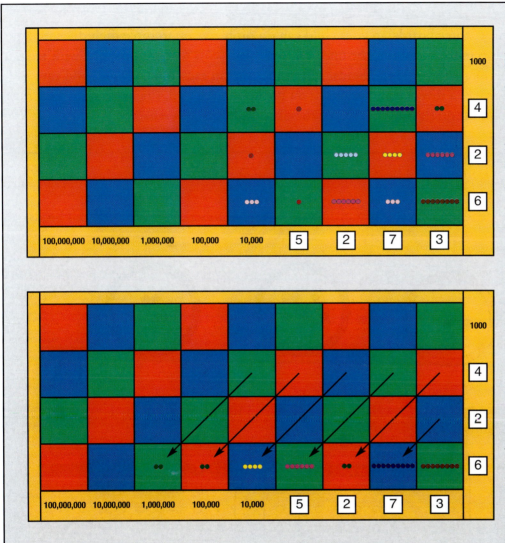

Next, she calculates the partial products, counting up the beads in each square and exchanging for the next hierarchy as needed. The partial products are represented in each of the horizontal rows as shown here. In this example, the bottom row represents 5273 x 6, and the answer is 31,638. The middle row represents 5273 x 20, and the answer is 105,460. The top row represents 5273 x 400, and the answer is 2,109,200 - not 21,092 moved over two spaces as we learned in the good old days!

To get the final answer, your child simply "slides and combines," adding together the tens, hundreds, thousands, etc. After she adds together the resulting combinations of beads, she can read the final answer – 2,246,298 - across the bottom of the checkerboard.

The final operation is division. Your child has already learned the process of division with the Golden Beads and the Stamp Game. She can't do division with the bead frames without taking them apart to distribute the beads!

So, to do long division problems with multi-digit divisors, she uses the test tube division materials or "racks and tubes." These consist of racks of test tubes, each holding colored beads in groups of ten, with green for units, blue for tens, red for hundreds, green for units of thousands…up to green again for millions. The beads are used to represent the dividend.

To represent the divisor, there are three boards, so your child can do problems up to three-digit divisors. The board with the green strip across the top represents units, the one with blue represents tens, and the one with red represents hundreds. Each board is perforated to hold the beads, with up to nine in each row, so your child can distribute the dividend evenly. If she makes a row of hundred beads on the hundred board, she needs to make a row of tens on the ten board, and a row of units on the unit board, for the distribution to be even.

Take the sample problem, 1,296 divided by 324:

Your child represents the dividend of 1,296 by putting the correct number of properly colored beads in matching colored bowls.

She shows the divisor of 324 by putting markers on three boards - three on the hundred board, two on the ten board, and four on the unit board.

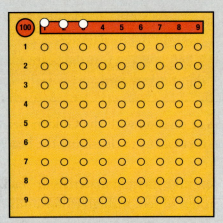 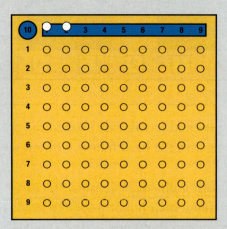 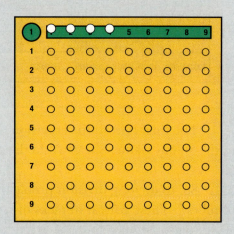

Then she distributes beads from the bowls, making exchanges as necessary so everybody gets a fair share. In this case, she can't distribute the thousand bead since there is only one, so she exchanges it for 10 hundreds and distributes the resulting 12 hundreds on the red, hundred board. For every row of hundreds on this board, the tens board gets tens and the unit board units:

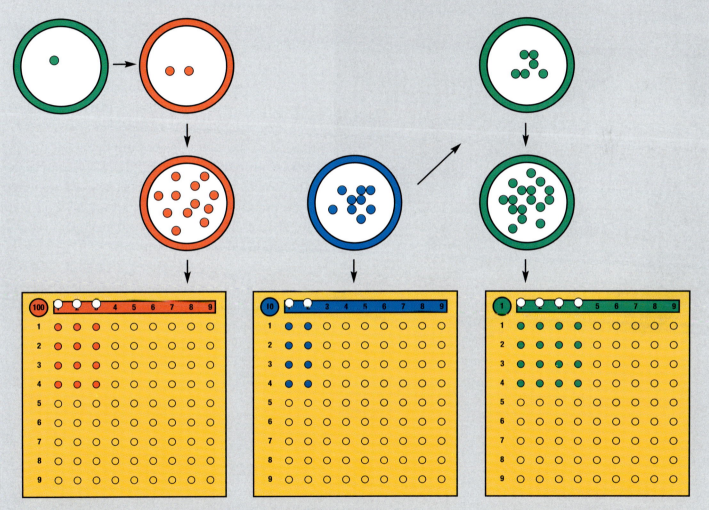

When she distributes the tens, there is one left over, so she exchanges it for ten units and then distributes the units. The answer in a division problem is always what one unit gets, which in this case is 4. If there had been any leftover beads in any of the bowls, that would represent the remainder.

With all of the materials shown above, your child can learn how to do very advanced addition, subtraction, multiplication and division problems with whole numbers. And, in each case, it is the concrete materials that provide her the key to understanding the process.

These materials all allow for the calculation of multi-digit problems with very little more difficulty than single-digit problems dependent on memorization of the tables. Instead of relying on memory to solve problems, your child uses the materials to solve problems - arriving at a better understanding of the process of addition, subtraction, multiplication and division than would be possible simply by relying on memorized combinations.

This is helping to build the mathematical mind that Maria Montessori talked about, going beyond merely getting a right answer to real understanding.

Memorization for the Four Operations

At this point you may be thinking, "That's all fine, but my child can't take the stamp game or the checkerboard with her into a test or to the checkout counter at the grocery store! When will she learn to get the right answers 'in her head' without the materials?"

The materials bring your child right up to the point of abstraction. What is necessary to take the final step is to memorize those tables that we all learned in school before we even did any problems. We learned the tables first, and then we applied them to problems; in Montessori, your child learns the process first and then memorizes her tables to make her work quicker. The order of learning is different, but the outcome is the same. However, the benefits of the Montessori approach are far superior - something we will take up in later chapters of this book.

So, while your child is learning how to add, subtract, multiply and divide with those concrete materials described above, she is doing parallel work with other materials to learn her "math facts." No flash cards required!

One of the first tools for learning the addition tables is the "strip board." By taking random problems out of the box of materials, without the answers, your child figures out the answers for herself and, in the process, begins to learn the combinations contained in those tables.

Here is what a few combinations look like on the addition strip board:

Do 10 of those per day for a few weeks and your child will be well on her way to memorizing her addition "facts." There is a similar "strip board" to learn the subtraction tables.

There are no strip boards for multiplication and division, but each process has its own board with perforations that allow your child to lay beads out and figure out the answers to various combinations.

When your child gets tired of doing these boards there are lots of other games to play to learn her math facts, starting with a series of "finger boards."

The next chart eliminates the duplicate combinations that your child really doesn't have to memorize once she understands the commutative property - e.g. 6 + 7 = 7 + 6. In all, there are four addition finger boards, the last one a "bingo board" with no numbers on it to put your child's knowledge of their addition facts to a real test.

There are similar finger boards for subtraction, multiplication and division as well.

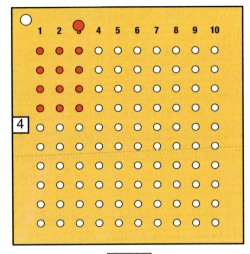

The multiplication board, with a sample combination of 4 x 3:

4 x 3 =

The first addition finger board, with the combination 6 + 7 = 13:

But there's still more - including the addition "snake game." Your child takes two color-coded bead bars at a time from a colored snake and turns them into golden ten bars whenever the sum is higher than 10.

Here is the setup of a sample problem, with the triangle of "reminder bars" on the side of the problem to record sums over ten:

1)   8 + 4 + 7 + 3 + 5 =

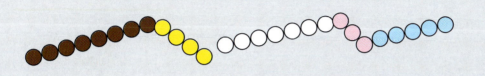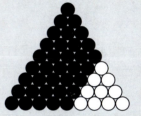

2) She brings down two bead bars at a time in order to add them together. In the sample problem shown here, she starts by bringing down the eight bar and the four bar.

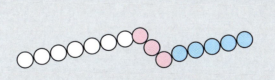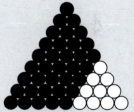

3) She performs the first addition of 8 + 4 = 12, and she substitutes a ten bar and a two reminder bar into the colored snake:

 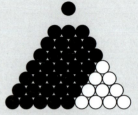

4) Then, in the next step, she takes down the combination 2 + 7 –

 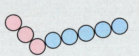 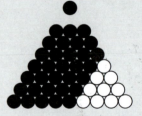

5) When she calculates the answer, she substitutes the 9 reminder bar into the colored snake:

 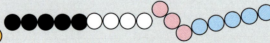 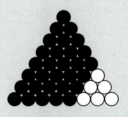

6) By calculating the remaining combinations, 9 + 3 and 2 + 5, she makes her final snake, with the answer, 27:

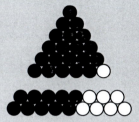

What makes this work worthwhile for your child is not just that she got the right answer, but rather all the combinations of numbers she had to calculate to get the final answer – helping her learn her addition combinations or "facts" in the context of a game rather than having to commit them by brute memory.

Even more challenging is the subtraction snake game, which not only helps her learn her subtraction facts but also prepares her to work with positive and negative integers. It's a lot more fun to play a "snake game" than learn addition and subtraction tables from flash cards!

For multiplication memorization, there are even more exercises and materials to play with to learn the tables. One of the most familiar is the bead cabinet, a collection of long and short chains in multiples of 1-10. She uses these, with accompanying numbered arrows, to "skip count" - which gives her multiples of the numbers 1-10 (the answers on the multiplication tables).

The final arrow is wider than the others, to indicate that this is the square of the number 4. The long bead chain allows your child to skip count all the way to the cube of the number 4, or all the multiples up to 64.

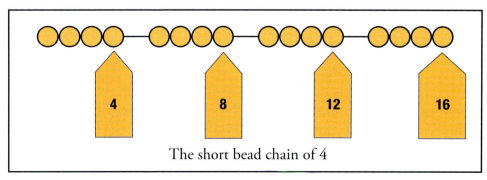

The short bead chain of 4

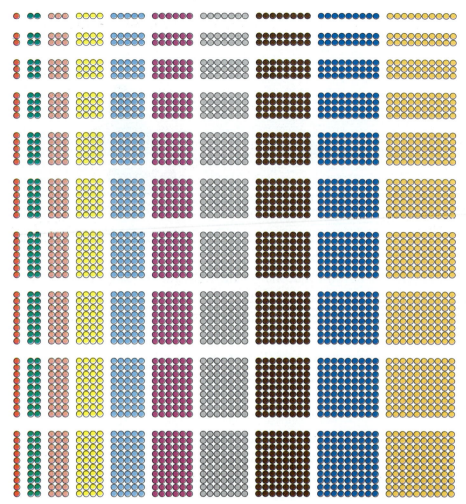

Yet another activity that helps your child learn her multiplication tables is the decanomial square - $(1 + 2 + 3 + 4 + 5 + 6 + 7 + 8 + 9 + 10)^2$ - which, in effect, is a physical representation of all the multiplication combinations she needs to memorize. She builds the square by multiplying 1 times 1, 2, 3, 4, 5…, then 2 times 1, 2, 3, 4, 5…etc. through 10 times 10. This forms a geometric pattern of beads in the shape of rectangles anchored by a diagonal spine of squares.

The most impressive part of this activity for your child is that the layout of the decanomial square can be transformed into a tower of cubes of the numbers 1-10. Simply combine the rectangles on the two sides of each square so they form squares themselves, combine the squares into cubes, and stack the cubes from biggest to smallest. That jogs her memory back to age three and the pink tower.

The bottom line is that there are many activities in a Montessori classroom that help your child learn her addition, subtraction, multiplication and division tables. This gives her a lot of choices and allows her to learn her math facts without the burden of memorization.

Fractions and the Four Operations

After your child is introduced to fractions and equivalent fractions, she is taught how to do simple calculations (addition and subtraction) with fractions having the same denominator. The concrete materials used for these activities are the "fraction circles," a set of metal insets that teach your child 1/2 through 1/10.

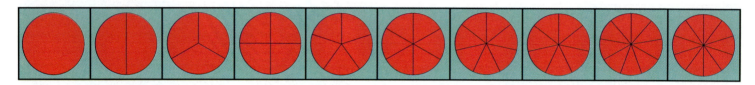

Later, your child uses larger sets of loose plastic materials - so she can make mixed numbers - to learn how to add, subtract, multiply and divide any fractions. But, instead of just teaching her rules, she manipulates the materials on sample problems to discover the rules for herself.

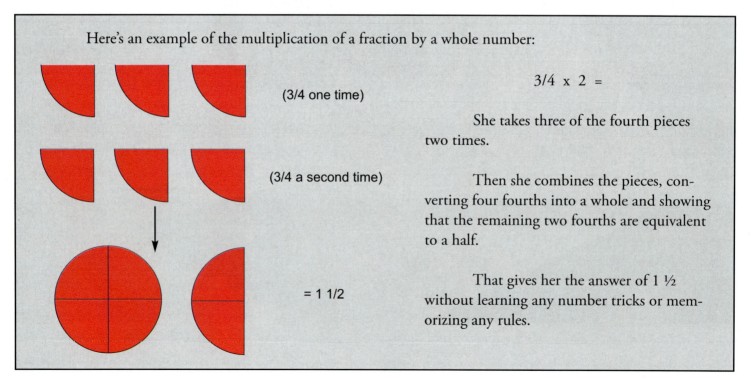

Here's an example of the multiplication of a fraction by a whole number:

(3/4 one time)

(3/4 a second time)

= 1 1/2

3/4 x 2 =

She takes three of the fourth pieces two times.

Then she combines the pieces, converting four fourths into a whole and showing that the remaining two fourths are equivalent to a half.

That gives her the answer of 1 ½ without learning any number tricks or memorizing any rules.

If your child does several problems with materials as a guide, she eventually discovers that she can simply multiply the numerator by the whole number and reduce the answer by combining the parts into equivalent fractions or mixed numbers. That's the rule, but nobody needs to tell her how to do it. The materials tell her what to do!

She can use the same procedure with all the rest of fraction problems - addition and subtraction of fractions with different denominators, multiplication of a fraction by a fraction, division of a fraction by a whole number or another fraction, and all the possible combinations of problems with mixed numbers as well.

Decimal Fractions and the Four Operations

Your child learns how to count in decimals, or decimal fractions, with numbers going into the millionths or sixth place after the decimal point. She creates the numbers with colored beads for whole numbers and flattened discs (or small cubes) with progressively lighter colors for the decimal fractions from tenths to millionths.

Then, she learns how to add, subtract, multiply and divide with decimals.

Here is an example of an addition problem: 235.0532 + 1234.2426 =   1,469.2958

Your child creates the first number on the board, putting the required quantities in the proper hierarchical space. She does the same with the second number. Than she merely adds them together - as she did with the stamp game - starting with the smallest hierarchy (in this case, the ten thousandths) and makes any exchanges necessary when she reaches ten in any hierarchy (there are no exchanges in this problem).

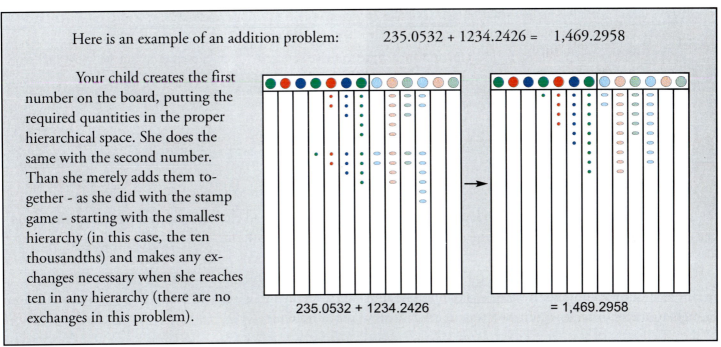

235.0532 + 1234.2426   = 1,469.2958

With this material, addition and subtraction are no more complicated for your child than the process of adding and subtracting whole numbers with the stamp game. Multiplication only becomes slightly more complicated when there are multi-digit multipliers with decimals in them. Division uses skittles to indicate the divisor, as with the stamp game, but there are special skittles to represent decimal divisors.

In addition to the hierarchical board depicted above, there is also a decimal checkerboard that is used to teach multiplication so your child can see for herself where the decimal goes in the answer.

Powers of Numbers

Your child is introduced to the concept of exponents and the powers of numbers with the use of the bead cabinet in the most concrete way. Take, for example, the short bead chain of 3. She can easily change it into a "square" of 3, which is the concrete representation of 3^2 or "3 x 3" or 9.

Then, she takes the long bead chain and turns it into three squares, which can then be stacked together to make a three "cube," the concrete representation of 3^3 or "3 x 3 x 3" or 27.

The same procedure can be followed with all the long and short bead chains, from 1 to 10. This introduces the child to the squares and cubes of the numbers she needs to know in her head.

Once the pattern is established with squares and cubes, your child recognizes that the exponent notation means to multiply a number by itself a certain number of times. She can then use this knowledge for the calculation of higher powers or for scientific notation in other areas of the curriculum.

Squaring

In my teaching experience, nothing is likely to excite, challenge and intellectually satisfy your child as much as the series of activities she does to learn how to extract square roots and cube roots. Moreover, these are wonderful examples of activities that develop the mathematical mind of your child the way Montessori envisioned. The activity for squaring and square roots involves a simple material called the "pegboard" and colored pegs to put in the holes.

Your child begins her work in this area by building squares on the pegboard. Here's an example of the square of a trinomial or three-digit number. The pegs are concrete representations of the parts of the trinomial square, representing 234^2.

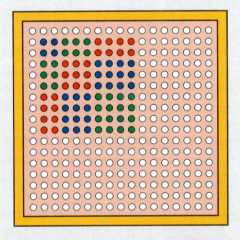

The layout on the pegboard clearly shows a pattern of squares and rectangles, and each part is a visual representation of the actual value:

- 200 x 200 = 40,000 or the blue square (upper left corner)
- 200 x 30 = 6,000 or the green rectangle (middle top)
- 200 x 4 = 800 or the red rectangle (top right corner)
- 200 x 30 = 6,000 or the green rectangle (left side middle)
- 30 x 30 = 900 or the red square (middle of middle set of rows)
- 30 x 4 = 120 or the blue rectangle (right side middle)
- 200 x 4 = 800 or the red rectangle (bottom left corner)
- 30 x 4 = 120 or the blue rectangle (bottom middle)
- 4 x 4 = 16 or the green square (lower right corner)

Add all these partial products together and you get the final answer, 54,756.

$234^2 = (200 + 30 + 4)^2 =$

(200 x 200) + (200 x 30) + (200 x 4) +
square   rectangle   rectangle
40,000   6,000   800

(200 x 30) + (30 x 30) + (30 x 4) +
rectangle   square   rectangle
6,000   900   120

(200 x 4) + (30 x 4) + (4 x 4) =
rectangle   rectangle   square
800   120   16

After your child has done a number of these problems, she eventually recognizes that the pattern is always the same and she can generalize the pattern into an algebraic equation:

$$(a + b + c)^2 =$$
$$a^2 + 2ab + 2ac + b^2 + 2bc + c^2$$

This is not an equation she is asked to memorize - it's one she discovers on her own and will likely remember a lot more easily than if her teacher gives it to her.

Square Root

Once your child has squared a lot of two- and three-digit numbers, she can find the square root of a given number by using the patterns she has learned, deconstructing the number into its parts.

Here is a sample problem to find the square root of 1,156:

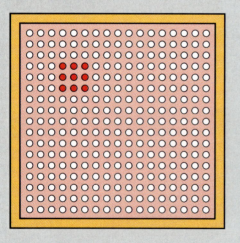

The square of the numbers 1-9 range from 1 to 81, while the square of 10-99 ranges from 100 to 9801. From this, your child discovers that a radicand with one or two digits yields a square root of one digit, while a radicand of three or four digits yields a square root of two digits.

So, in this example, with a radicand of 1,156, the square root will have to be a two-digit number. Your child begins her work with the first two digits in the radicand - one thousand, one hundred. She exchanges the thousand for 10 hundreds, and finds the biggest square she can make with the resulting 11 hundreds.

This gives her a square of 3 hundreds - which is the same as 30^2 or 900 (physically represented on the board by the 9 red, hundred pegs). That means the first digit of the square root is 3 tens.

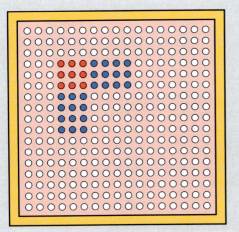

Next, with the leftover two hundreds turned into 20 tens and the original 5 tens, she has 25 tens (blue pegs). She researches the second digit of the root by constructing rectangles on two sides of the squares with the blue pegs, building in both directions equally. Since there are only enough tens to make a rectangle of four-wide on each side of the original square, this indicates that the second digit of the square root is probably 4. But it's not confirmed until the square is complete.

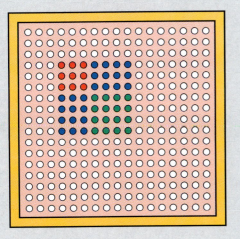

Finally, with the one leftover ten turned into 10 units and the original 6 units, she has a total of 16 units (green pegs). She uses these to build a square in the space between the two rectangles. This completes the larger square and confirms the second digit.

She can read the answer across the bottom of the resulting square - three tens and four units, or 34, which is the square root of the original number, 1,156. You can confirm the answer by adding up all the pegs on the board - 16 units, 24 tens, and 9 hundreds - which total 1,156.

Finding a square root with the materials as shown above is a lot more complicated than punching a few numbers on a calculator, but that's the whole point of the process - to let your child think her way through the problem.

The same procedure can be followed for finding a three-digit root from a 5- or 6-digit number. And my students always tried to make the problems as complicated as they could to increase the level of challenge!

Cubing and Cube Root

The study of cube roots begins much the same way as square roots - your child builds cubes with the "cubing materials" - cubes from 1-10 and multiple squares from 1-10. She builds binomial and trinomial cubes to see what parts are involved.

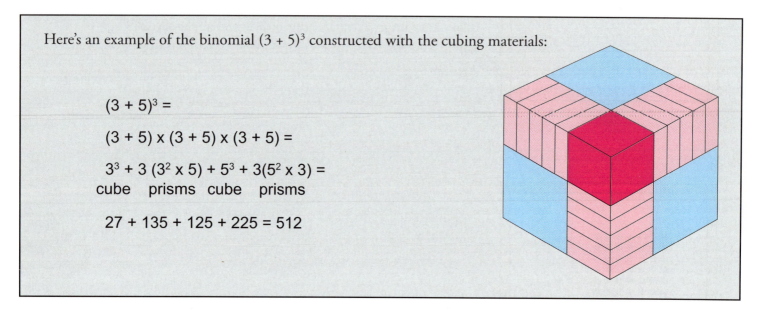

Here's an example of the binomial $(3 + 5)^3$ constructed with the cubing materials:

$(3 + 5)^3 =$

$(3 + 5) \times (3 + 5) \times (3 + 5) =$

$\underset{\text{cube}}{3^3} + \underset{\text{prisms}}{3(3^2 \times 5)} + \underset{\text{cube}}{5^3} + \underset{\text{prisms}}{3(5^2 \times 3)} =$

$27 + 135 + 125 + 225 = 512$

After building several binomial cubes, your child discovers that they always follow the pattern of the binomial cube familiar to her from her days in the primary class, combining cubes and rectangular prisms in the same fashion as a puzzle at that level.

This leads her to a study of the trinomial cube - again a familiar material from the primary class. This cube is a concrete representation of the following algebraic equation:

$(a + b + c)^3 = a^3 + 3a^2b + 3a^2c + b^3 + 3ab^2 + 3b^2c + c^3 + 3ac^2 + 3bc^2 + 6abc$

If a represents 100s, b represents 10s and c represents units, then the trinomial cube becomes a guide for your child to extract the cube root of a number as large as nine digits. She deconstructs the number into its parts of the cube, much the way she proceeded when she did the square root work. And she's likely to have a great time doing it!

Other math work to do with materials -

Your child uses concrete materials to learn these other math concepts and procedures:

- She uses the negative snake game to represent positive and negative integers and to learn the rules for their addition, subtraction, multiplication and division.

- She uses the checkerboard to work compound multiplication problems without having to use partial products, a process called "cross multiplication."

- She uses a special Montessori "centesimal" metal inset to translate fractions into percents.

- She uses modified number rods and a special bead frame to do calculations in various number bases.

Conclusion:

Consider that a lot of these more advanced concepts are not taught until middle school or high school in conventional schooling. Once you see your child work with these materials, it's hard not to be impressed by their sheer beauty and clarity in teaching math concepts.

Maria Montessori did not design these wonderful materials just to impress, however. Their purpose is to develop your child's mathematical mind, to allow her to build her brain power and, as an added benefit, to do well on tests. That's what we are going to look at in the next three chapters.

The first deals with the psychological and developmental rationale for having your child use the Montessori math materials; the next chapter deals with the facts of life from brain research to validate this approach to math; and the third looks at the issue of Montessori mathematics in the context of state standards and testing.

All three chapters will help you appreciate that the Montessori, materials-based approach is an effective and benefit-rich way for your child to learn mathematics.

Chapter 3
The Benefits of Montessori Math Materials

At this point, you may have the feeling that Montessori's concrete math materials are pretty neat, and you somehow know that they are better for your child than the way you (and I) learned arithmetic in school. However, you may not be able to explain why this is so. After all, why should your child need these materials to learn what we learned out of our textbooks and workbooks?

Your child can learn to do arithmetic problems from a textbook or from the Montessori materials, producing similar results as far as his ability to come up with the right answer. What makes the concrete materials more useful to him than the textbook? What are the developmental and pedagogical benefits that come from using materials?

Montessori Materials are Three-Dimensional and Multi-Sensory

The richness of the learning experience for your child depends on the number of senses and dimensions involved in the process. Montessori math materials are real, three-dimensional, multi-sensory objects instead of flat pictures in a book or, worse, just words and numbers to explain mathematical concepts.

Consider the difference between having your child look at a picture of a cube and holding one in his hand. Your child can see the cube's size and color (visual), feel its texture (touch), hear it named a "thousand cube" by the teacher (sound), compare its weight to the bead in the other hand (perception of mass), experience its three-dimensionality ("stereognostic" sense - or the mental perception of depth), turn it over to see it from all sides (movement and stereoscopic vision), count the beads from every angle (numerical sense), see how many faces it has (geometric or spatial sense), even feel the coolness of the beads in his hand (temperature sensibility). All of these are different ways of "sensing" or perceiving the cube, and together they stimulate the learning process and enhance recall through memory.

Contrast that with the picture in this book. It's a flat, two-dimensional representation of a real cube, understandable only because the human eye and adult conventions recognize perspective in a flat drawing to make it look like a three-dimensional object. You can only "see" three faces of this six-faced object. It could never be as useful to your child for learning as the actual cube from the golden bead materials.

All of the Montessori math materials have this advantage for learning. They are all concrete, multi-sensory objects. Consider, for example, the green-blue-red designation for units-tens-hundreds of the stamp game, bead frames, checkerboard, and division boards. And then there are the three-dimensional shapes of the parts of the binomial and trinomial cubes (shown here).

Every material provides an enriched learning experience for your child.

Montessori Materials are "Manipulatives"

Most of the educational world has recognized the effectiveness of children learning with hands-on materials or "manipulatives" rather than as passive recipients of lecture, textbook and chalkboard explanations. In the area of mathematics, there are educational supply companies that produce materials that look like some of the materials used in Montessori classrooms for nearly 100 years. Unfortunately, even with the knowledge that "hands-on" learning is better, the use of manipulatives is limited in most classrooms in our society, and even then they are most commonly used as a prop for the teacher rather than something to be used by the student.

Montessori adopted an approach to education that uses a "three-period lesson" that puts the emphasis on the activity of your child as the heart of learning. For the first period, the simplest example is to show him several objects and name them: "This is a unit bead. This is a ten bar. This is a hundred square." In the second period, we ask him, "Show me the hundred square. Show me the ten bar. Show me the unit bead." Finally, in the third period, we point to each object in turn and ask, "What is this?"

The first period is the gift of the teacher to your child, the lesson (association). The second period is when we ask your child to do something, to practice what he has learned (recognition). The third period verifies that he has, in fact, learned what he was taught in the first period (recall).

Montessori believed that the second period is the most important stage of learning for your child. During this time he internalizes a new piece of information or a new concept by taking an active role and doing something himself.

In the case of the math materials outlined in the previous chapter, your child really learns most during the time he spends handling the materials himself. No matter how good the teacher and how clearly she explains new concepts, your child will not really understand until he puts his hands on the materials and manipulates them himself. (This is true even for adults, as we see repeatedly when we give presentations to our teacher-trainees and watch them nod in affirmation that they understand - only to discover that they didn't "really" understand until later when they practiced with the materials themselves).

One of the reasons we know this is true is because of the connection between movement and cognition that research of recent decades has documented.

Angeline Lillard, a developmental psychologist at the University of Virginia, has collected hundreds of research studies that validate basic Montessori principles of teaching. The first of the principles she examines is the importance of movement in learning. "In sum," she writes, "there is abundant research showing that movement and cognition are closely intertwined. People represent spaces and objects more accurately, remember information better, and show superior social cognition when their movements are aligned with what they are thinking about or learning. Traditional classrooms are not set up to capitalize on the relationship between movement and cognition. In contrast, Montessori has movement at its core."[11]

In other words, it's not just more interesting or fun for your child to learn with the materials - it's more effective.

---

[11] Lillard, Angeline Stoll. Montessori: The Science Behind the Genius, New York: Oxford University Press, 2005. p. 56.

One of the studies she cites involves the use of an abacus to learn mathematics - a device similar in many ways to the Montessori bead frames. "Children who are more expert at using the abacus are more proficient at solving math problems, even when they are not using the abacus."[12]

In speaking of the Montessori math materials, in particular, Lillard notes, "Many Montessori materials are designed to expose the child's hand to abstract concepts, which are then gradually revealed to the mind."[13]

Maria Montessori, using only the observational techniques of what she called "scientific pedagogy," discovered this connection between movement and learning long before these later research studies validated her findings. She was particularly impressed with the power of the human hand to express the highest capabilities of the human spirit, dedicating an entire chapter of *The Absorbent Mind* to the idea.[14]

---

[12] Ibid. p. 53, citing Stigler, J.W. (1984) "Mental abacus": The effect of abacus training on Chinese children's mental calculation. *Educational Psychologist*, 35 (2), 87-100.

[13] Ibid. p. 67.

[14] Montessori, Maria. *The Absorbant Mind.* Dell Publishing: New York. 1984. "Intelligence and the Hand," p. 151-159.

Montessori Materials Promote Active, Discovery Learning

Another important characteristic of Montessori materials, closely related to the issue of movement described above, is that they promote active rather than passive learning in your child. This is discovery by the child instead of spoon feeding by the teacher.

A simple example of this is the memorization work. Instead of giving your child lists of math facts with answers to memorize - the addition, subtraction, multiplication and division tables - he uses the strip boards, bead boards or the finger boards to find the answers himself. That produces a major difference in motivation for the learning process. Your child is much more likely to be drawn to an activity that asks him to figure something out himself than to simply memorize something a teacher tells him he should learn.

At a more advanced level, your child can use the fraction materials to discover for himself the rules for calculating with fractions. He can learn the algebraic formula for the cubing of a binomial by assembling a binomial cube himself and then taking it apart to analyze the pieces.

The more active and in control your child is, the better the end result. In a Montessori classroom, rather than passively following the directions of the teacher, your child makes his own choices throughout the day that feed his thirst for knowledge and intellectual growth. Teachers usually don't have to tell him, "It's time to do an addition problem with the stamp game now." He takes the materials off the shelf when he chooses to practice what he learned in an earlier lesson. He is in control.

This fits nicely with Lillard's second principle of Montessori education, "that learning and well-being are improved when people have a sense of control over their lives."[15] Summing up the research to back up this principle, she says, "the provision of choice is associated with several positive consequences. People learn and remember better, solve tasks better, and opt to engage in tasks more and longer when they think they have more control."[16]

Later in this chapter, she talks about how research validates the Montessori approach of giving your child limited choices, or free choice within boundaries. "There is a point at which having too many choices becomes negative and works against people's sense of control."[17]

After a lesson on stamp game addition, for example, your child is expected to do some follow up work on his own (that "second period" we talked about earlier). However, the teacher may allow him to make up his own problems, he can choose when to do this work versus his other work in the class, and he may even decide for himself how many problems he needs to do to master this particular skill.

Learning is an *activity* on the part of your child that allows him to *discover* new knowledge - not something infused into a passive and receptive head by a diligent teacher.

---

[15] Ibid. p. 29.
[16] Ibid. p. 86.
[17] Ibid. p. 94.

Montessori Materials Encourage Collaborative Learning

Another advantage of the Montessori math materials is that they allow your child to work with others. There's rarely a chance for several students to collaborate on a problem from a textbook or on a worksheet. Copying someone else's answer is not an authentic learning process! But the materials lend themselves to cooperative learning, which is quite a different and more fruitful experience.

In a simple addition problem with the golden bead materials, for example, one student can give out the numbers, two other students can take trays to get the quantities in beads, another student can put the quantities together to get the answer, that yet another student can record on a dry erase board. That's as many as five children "collaborating" - working together - to get the answer. Your child can choose any of those roles, eventually rotating into an experience of all five.

With more advanced materials, like the checkerboard, students can take turns putting out the bead bars for the partial products. With the test tube division materials, each of three students can take one of the boards to put the beads on as the problem progresses. With the cube root work, each step of the problem - or each piece of the binomial or trinomial cube - can be figured out by a different student or two students taking turns.

Your child can work alone with the materials, or he can use them with small groups of his peers (obviously, there is a problem if the number gets too big to be efficient or to allow full participation by all the students involved). The materials are usually a lot more fun to use when two or three students work together, which fits nicely with the critical social development of students at elementary ages.

But there's more involved than the gains in socialization - important as those gains may be. Collaboration actually produces better learning for your child. This appears to be true whether your child takes the lead role or he follows the lead of others, since both leaders and followers benefit from the collaboration.

Once again, there is extensive educational and developmental research that confirms this conclusion.

"Children in Montessori classrooms have ample opportunity for learning by imitating models, through peer tutoring, and in collaboration," writes Lillard. She adds: "Research in schools and psychology laboratories has shown that learning occurs in these situations. Furthermore, peer tutoring and collaborative arrangements are superior to traditional whole-class teaching in terms both of the learning and the social climate that they support."[18]

Working together is actually a better way for your child to learn.

Montessori Materials are Self-Correcting

When Montessori developed her teaching materials, she often did so in a way that they were self-correcting or at least allowed your child to check his own work - something she called "control of error."[19] A typical example of this at the primary level is the cylinder blocks - your child can only put the knobbed cylinders back in the blocks one way for them all to fit.

Many of the Montessori materials for mathematics have this same characteristic. When your child makes an exchange of 10 ten bars for a 100 square, the materials themselves match in size and shape at the point that an exchange needs to be made. When he does an addition snake game, he can check to see if the original bead bars match the final answer or not. Two equivalent fractions fit exactly into the same space within the fraction circle. Constructing a trinomial cube can only be done with the pattern that represents the algebraic formula for a trinomial cube.

---

[18] Ibid. p. 223.
[19] Montessori. *Absorbent Mind*. "Mistakes and their Correction." p. 241-247.

The materials themselves frequently tell your child whether he is on the right track to solve a problem or has arrived at the correct answer (as in the spindle boxes shown here). This is a huge psychological benefit for him.

Consider the emotional and psychological impact on your child if he works hard on a problem, only to have a teacher tell him he made a mistake and got the wrong answer - making a red mark on his workbook paper. This breeds loss of self-confidence, discouragement and reluctance to do the work again. Contrast that to a situation where your child works hard on a problem, discovers for himself that he made a mistake, and uses the materials to retrace his steps and correct his own error. This produces increased self-esteem, encouragement and the incentive to do the work again. Not all materials are self-correcting. Then, you might ask, shouldn't teachers check your child's work to make sure he gets the right answers? Not really.

When I mentor teachers, I always encourage them to avoid checking student work as much as possible. That may seem strange to you as a parent, and teachers are sometimes self-conscious about letting mistakes slip through on work sent home with your child for fear that it will reflect badly on them as teachers.

For those materials that aren't self-correcting, there can be answer sheets for prepared problems in the classroom. In other subject areas, such as History or Biology, Montessori practice usually provides a *control booklet* that allows your child to check his own work. It should be no different for math problems - answer sheets are just the equivalent of control booklets for math problems.

Or, if your child is given the choice of making up his own problems, it's fairly simple to teach him how to use a calculator to check his own work.

But, you ask, won't that allow him to *cheat* and find the answer or correct a wrong answer without really doing the work? That's where *observation* becomes important as an assessment tool. If teachers are observing instead of burying their noses in papers all day, they will notice when your child takes shortcuts - and have a brief talk about making sure he is learning something when he does his work.

Observation is a more important assessment tool than checking answers anyway. If your child spends a half hour or more with the test tube division materials doing a very long and complicated problem with a dividend into the millions and a three-digit divisor, checking the answer only tells the teacher whether it's right or wrong - with no indication of where he went wrong.

If, on the other hand, the teacher spends time observing, she may notice that he exchanged a leftover 100 for only 9 tens - or that he took the extra 10 tens without giving up the 100 in exchange. Those are two quite different mistakes, and an observant teacher can call your child's attention to what's important.

Furthermore, when a teacher or classroom assistant checks every problem your child does, it gives him the message that his work doesn't really count until it's checked by an adult. This undermines your child's independence, prevents him from learning to self-evaluate (metacognition), takes over control of the learning process, and makes him dependent on external rewards or recognition for self-validation. Self-esteem, independence, responsibility for oneself, and intrinsic motivation are all more important contributors to your child's ultimate success in life.

Montessori Materials are Geometric Representations of Abstract Concepts

A final, striking characteristic of Montessori materials is that they are usually designed as geometric representations of mathematical concepts, arithmetical processes or, at the highest level of abstraction, algebraic generalizations. In other words, they allow your child to have a visual reinforcement of some of the most abstract concepts.

Consider, for example, the golden beads. The unit bead is comparable to a point in geometry, the ten bar to a line, the hundred square to a surface, and the thousand cube to a solid. These "fundamental concepts" of the Montessori *geometry* curriculum are used to represent and concretize the number concepts of decimal numeration in *mathematics*.

The checkerboard is another good example. It is nothing but a geometric pattern and visual representation of the rules for compound multiplication. Look back at the illustration in Chapter 2 and note that the intersection of unit times unit produces a unit in the product, while the intersection of ten thousands times hundreds, for example, produces millions in the product.

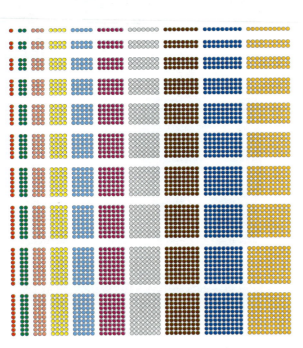

The decanomial square is not only a geometric representation of the problem $(1 + 2 + 3 + 4 + 5 + 6 + + 8 + 9 + 10)^2$ but your child can also transform it into $(a + b + c + d + e + f + g + h + i + j)^2$ to produce the algebraic formula for a decanomial square:

(squares)   (rectangles)
a^2 + $2ab$ + $2ac$ + $2ad$ + $2ae$ + $2af$ + $2ag$ + $2ah$ + $2ai$ + $2aj$ +
b^2 + $2bc$ + $2bd$ + $2be$ + $2bf$ + $2bg$ + $2bh$ + $2bi$ + $2bj$ +
c^2 + $2cd$ + $2ce$ + $2cf$ + $2cg$ + $2ch$ + $2ci$ + $2cj$ +
d^2 + $2de$ + $2df$ + $2dg$ + $2dh$ + $2di$ + $2dj$ +
e^2 + $2ef$ + $2eg$ + $2eh$ + $2ei$ + $2ej$ +
f^2 + $2fg$ + $2fh$ + $2fi$ + $2fj$ +
g^2 + $2gh$ + $2gi$ + $2gj$ +
h^2 + $2hi$ + $2hj$ +
i^2 + $2ij$ +
j^2

Each term of the formula is represented in concrete form by a square or a rectangle in the geometric pattern of the decanomial square. The geometry symbolizes the number pattern and leads to your child's discovery of this fairly complex algebraic formula - and it could easily be your 9-year-old doing this kind of algebra!

Binomial and trinomial squares are constructed with regular patterns of squares and rectangles that lead to discovery of the algebraic formula. This allows the extraction of square roots from numbers into six digits.

Perhaps the most striking example of how Montessori uses geometry to illustrate, lead to understanding and allow complex mathematical calculations is the work with cube roots. The binomial cube (see illustration on page 32) is the physical representation of the parts - terms - of a two-digit number cubed. The trinomial cube, as pointed out in the same chapter, is a concrete, geometric representation of the algebraic formula:

$$(a + b + c)^3 = a^3 + 3a^2b + 3a^2c + b^3 + 3ab^2 + 3b^2c + c^3 + 3ac^2 + 3bc^2 + 6abc$$

This link between geometrical representations and mathematical calculation is embedded in Montessori math materials, reinforced by a strong and very advanced study of geometry, and is an important reason for the success of the math materials.

Conclusion:

All of these psychological and developmental benefits contribute to the growth of your child's mathematical mind.

His mind is fed by the three-dimensional, multi-sensory nature of the materials, the way he is able to handle and move them around, the discoveries he makes from that manipulation, the collaborative learning that he can engage in through the materials, the self-correcting he can do under their guidance, and the geometric visualization he gets to reinforce his abstract understanding. All of this makes learning with materials so much more effective than textbook-based learning.

But that's not all! These materials actually help him develop a more powerful brain. That's the focus of the next chapter.

Chapter 4
Montessori Math and the Human Brain

When Maria Montessori wrote about developing the child's mathematical mind, she didn't have the advantage of modern brain science. She observed children as a scientist to develop her mathematical materials and her educational method, anticipating many of the benefits confirmed by developmental psychology and educational research as outlined in the previous chapter. However, there simply weren't the tools available to unlock the secrets of the human brain that we enjoy today.

Today, scientists can study the human brain as it functions with new imaging devices. Magnetic Resonance Imaging (MRI) machines provide cross-sectional images of the brain, or a "real-time image of blood-flow patterns, revealing what parts of the brain are active during particular tasks."[20] In the early 1990s, MRI technology was enhanced by putting a series of pictures taken together close in time to produce "functional" MRI (fMRI) images that resemble a motion picture.

Yet another variation on MRI technology, Nuclear Magnetic Resonance Imaging (NMRI), "is 30,000 times faster and captures an image every 50 milliseconds."[21]

There are many other tools that have been developed in recent decades: Positron Emission Tomography (PET) scans, which trace radioactive substances as they move through the brain; spectrometers which measure the presence of neurotransmitters or brain chemicals; magnetoencephalography (MEG) readings, which are advanced versions of the older electroencephalogram (EEG) and which can detect the faint magnetic fields generated by the

---

[20] Howard, Pierce J. *The Owner's Manual for the Brain*: Everyday Applications from Mind-Brain Research. Bard Press, Austin, TX 2000. p. 53.
[21] Jensen, Eric. *Teaching with the Brain in Mind*. Association for Supervision and Curriculum Development, Alexandria, VA, 1998. p. 2.

brain's neural network; and computerized axial tomography (CAT) scans, a 1970s era technology that can take cross-sectional pictures of the brain.

Although the science of the brain is, in many ways, still in its infancy - and these tools haven't become so common as to be used to scan your child's brain while she uses the stamp game - scientists have learned an enormous amount about the human brain in the half century since Maria Montessori's death. This new knowledge, which exploded in the 1990s, can shed light on why Montessori math materials are so effective in teaching your child.

The Anatomy of the Brain

Your child was born with a brain containing some 100 billion neurons - give or take a few billion! During her life, her brain will double or even triple in size. But it's not the size of her brain or the number of neurons that will determine how smart she will be. It's how her brain creates connections as she grows up that makes the difference.

Let's go back to some fundamentals of anatomy to understand why this is true.

Each neuron in your child's brain consists of a cell body (the central processor), dendrites (the receivers or input end), and an axon (the transmitters or output end). Between one neuron and the next is a small space called a synapse, and information is transmitted across the synapse by an electro-chemical process.

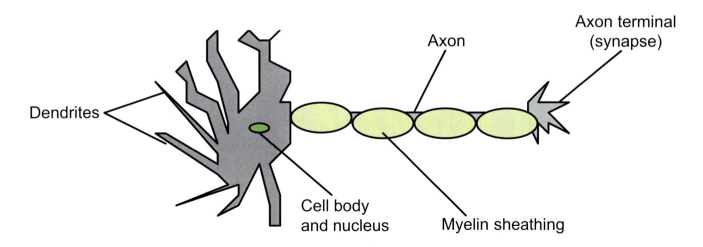

Put all the neurons together, and you have your child's brain - a brain that has a lot of very distinct parts. Let's do a quick tour of those parts.

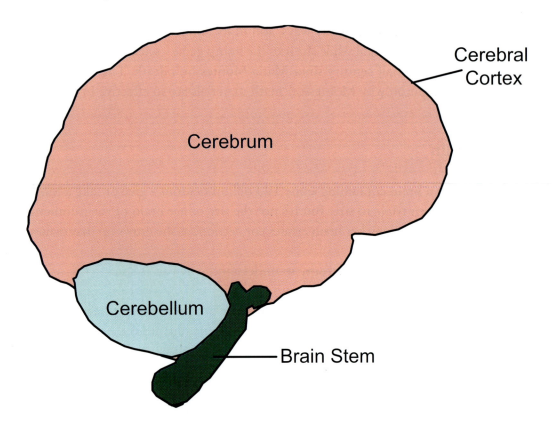

Starting from bottom to top, her brain is divided into brain stem, cerebellum, cerebrum and cerebral cortex.

The brain stem, sometimes referred to as the reptilian brain, is the most primitive part of her brain and controls bodily functions like respiration, digestion and circulation. The cerebellum, also called the "little brain," controls coordinated movement. The cerebrum, the largest part of the human brain, is the newest development in brain evolution and the thinking part of the brain. The cerebral cortex, the outer layer of the cerebrum, is the place where the most advanced human thinking takes place and where your child plans and makes choices.[22]

---

[22] All the sources cited in this chapter paint the same general picture of the brain's parts.

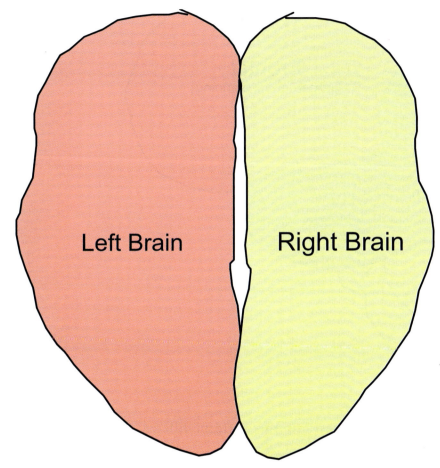

If you could examine your child's cerebrum, you would see that it is divided into a right and left hemisphere.

It has long been thought that the right hemisphere processes language and logic and the left side spatial and creative thinking, and there is still some basis to that division.[23]

However, it's much more complicated than that. Recent research has shown, for example, that new information and novel challenges are processed in the right hemisphere, while the left hemisphere handles already familiar information and familiar routines. [24]

---

[23] Howard, p. 48-49.
[24] Sylwester, Robert. *A Biological Brain in a Cultural Classroom: Enhancing Cognitive and Social Development Through Collaborative Classroom Management.* Corwin Press Inc.: Thousand Oaks, CA. 2nd Edition. 2003. p. 36.

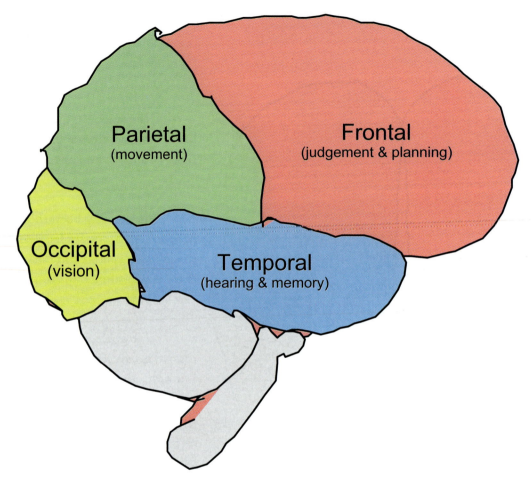

Each hemisphere of your child's cerebrum has lobes, or sections, that perform different functions. These are the occipital, parietal, temporal and frontal lobes.

The occipital lobe, in the middle back of the brain, is primarily responsible for vision. The parietal lobe, on the top of the brain, processes higher sensory input and plans for movement. The temporal lobes, on the sides near the ears, are primarily responsible for hearing and memory. The frontal lobe, behind the forehead, is involved with purposeful acts like judgment, creativity, problem solving and planning.[25]

---

[25] Jensen, p. 9.

The cerebral cortex, also called "gray matter" because of the general lack of insulating myelin that turns neurons white, is a folded, outer layer of the cerebrum. The cortex, too, has parts. There's a sensory part that receives the data from concrete experiences, a part that integrates these sensations through a process of reflection, a part that formulates an abstract hypothesis based on that reflection, and a part that prepares for action or testing of the hypothesis. These functions roughly correspond to the cycle of learning.[26]

The frontal cortex, located right behind the forehead and the part that formulates the abstract hypothesis, is thought to be the place of your child's most advanced thinking and problem solving. This is the part of the brain that most separates us from other species of animals.[27]

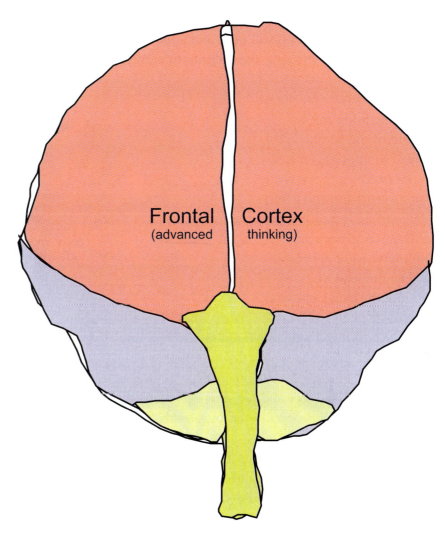

---

[26] Zull, James E. The Art of Changing the Brain: Enriching the Practice of Teaching by Exploring the Biology of Learning. Stylus Publishing: Sterling, VA. 2002. p. 34-37.
[27] All of the authors cited and numerous other sources converge on this point.

Brain Growth

Your child's brain will more than double in size during her life. But she won't double the number of neurons - in fact, she will inevitably lose millions or even billions of neurons as she grows up.

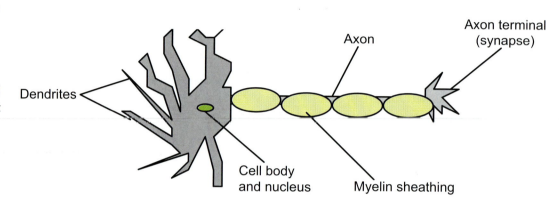

There are two factors that contribute to the growth of the human brain, related to opposite ends of the neuron - on the receiving end, neurons develop a forest of dendrites as they interact with other neurons and multiply new connections; at the other end of the neuron, the elongated axon develops a coating of "myelin," a fatty sheathing that acts like insulation, increasing the speed of electrical transmission along the axon and reducing interference from nearby neurons.

Both of these developments depend on how active a neuron becomes in the inner life of your child. When a neuron is activated repeatedly, it develops thousands of new dendritic connections to other neurons in her brain - and that activity is believed to be responsible for whether a neuron gets "myelinated."

A failure to use neurons in this active collaboration results in the loss of those neurons to her brain. Nature decides that, if she hasn't used neurons by the times of pruning, she probably won't need them. It's a sophisticated principle that neuroscientists have summed up succinctly: "Use it or lose it."

This "pruning" process goes on from shortly after birth to puberty. "The brain is literally customizing itself for your particular lifestyle from the day you're born. Soon after, the brain prunes away unneeded cells and billions of unused connections."[28]

---

[28] Jensen, p. 21.

By contrast, those neurons that are used repeatedly develop a multiplicity of dendrites on their receiving ends so they can make more connections. Through repeated stimulation, dendrites branch out and multiply connections to create "neural forests" which help your child reach a higher level of brain power and understanding.[29]

And all of this development is somewhat time sensitive. Research shows a spurt of dendritic branching in the right hemisphere between ages 4 and 7, in the left hemisphere between ages 9 and 12, with the full maturation of the neural bridge between them by the age of 13.[30]

It is this dendritic branching or formation of new neural networks that makes your child "smarter."

Learning as the Art of Building the Brain

Experts agree that your child's brain gets smarter by building more complex synaptic connections. The learning process builds a distinct architecture in her brain, hardwiring connections after repeated usage so that new neural networks become part of the capacity of her brain to solve problems in the future.

"It is not the number of neurons itself that determines our mental characteristics; it is how they are connected…Learning is defined as the establishment of new neural networks…It is the density of the brain as measured by the number of synapses that distinguishes greater from lesser mental capacity," writes Dr. Pierce Howard, director of research for the Center for Applied Cognitive Studies in Charlotte, NC.[31]

Eric Jensen, an internationally known educator who has taught at all levels from elementary through university, expresses a similar view. "The key to getting smarter is growing more synaptic connections between brain cells and not losing existing connections…The single best way to grow a better brain is through challenging problem solving. This creates new dendritic connections that allow us to make even more connections."[32]

Howard Zull, a professor of biology and Director of the University Center for Innovation in Teaching and Education at Case Western Reserve University, rates the effectiveness of teaching by the amount of change it produces in the architecture of the brain. "Teaching is the art of changing the brain…*creating conditions that lead to change in the learner's brain*. We can't get inside and rewire a brain, but we can arrange things so that it gets rewired."[33]

---

[29] Ibid. p. 35.
[30] Howard. p. 44.
[31] Jensen. p. 15 and 35.
[32] Zull. p. 5.

This all fits well with Maria Montessori's ideas about learning being a process of development within a prepared environment rather than the acquisition of a body of information or the memorization of factual information. She would have easily embraced the findings of modern neuroscience and applied those findings to the way your child learns.

In particular, her focus on the "mathematical mind" (cf. Chapter 1) would have been expressed more biologically if she had had access to the discoveries of brain research in recent decades.

So, now that we know a little bit about what modern science has learned about the brain and its parts, and how human brains go about the process of learning, how can we relate all this to the Montessori math program and materials?

Montessori Math and Brain Building -

This leads us to the central thesis of this book - that use of the Montessori math materials actually builds your child's brain. Three important points come to mind:

1. Montessori math materials engage all four lobes of her cerebrum simultaneously.

2. Montessori math materials connect the right and left hemispheres of her brain.

3. Montessori math materials actively engage the prefrontal cortex, the most "advanced" part of her brain.

Let's take a look at each of these ideas and examine the Montessori materials in light of these three concepts.

---

[33] Zull. p. 5.

1. The Four Lobes

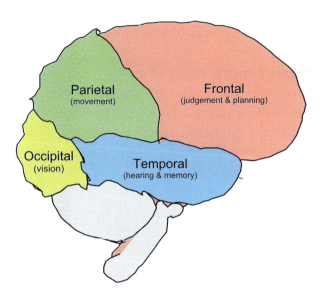

The concrete, multi-sensory, and manipulative nature of these materials (see Chapter 3) ensures that they simultaneously engage multiple areas of your child's brain, including all four lobes of her cerebrum.

Her occipital lobe sees the colors and shapes of the materials. Her temporal lobe takes in the auditory cues that accompany their use and triggers memory associations. Her parietal lobe is engaged in the purposeful movement of the materials. And her frontal lobe provides the problem-solving processing to put all the sensory input together and find a solution to the problem.

The simultaneous activation of all four lobes creates a multiplicity of neural connections and builds a network in your child's brain.

Contrast this to the typical "listen to the problem and grab an answer from your memory databank" approach to mathematics that depends on memorization rather than concrete experience and understanding. This depends almost exclusively on the memory center of the brain and is simply not as rich a brain-building experience as the Montessori materials-based approach.

Multi-sensory, experiential learning "contain data from all the senses at once, rather than just vision, or just sound. They are 'sense-luscious.'" says Zull.[34] Jensen goes so far as to say that "challenging sensory stimulation has been rightfully compared to a brain 'nutrient'."[35]

The production of new neural networks through use of Montessori math materials has an impact on the permanent wiring of the brain that will be available as your child gets older and uses her brain for analytical thinking and problem-solving.

---

[34] Zull. p. 145.
[35] Jensen. p. 31.

2. Right and Left Hemispheres

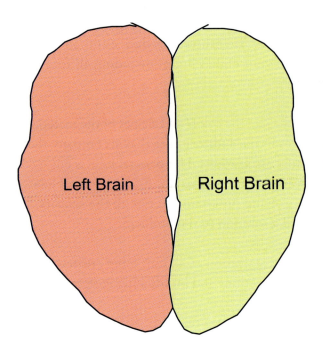

Montessori materials also activate the neural connections between the right and left hemispheres of your child's brain.

The use of geometric shapes to represent arithmetical, or even algebraic, processes (see p. 43-45) ensures that your child engages both sides of her brain as she works to solve a math problem. Her right brain is activated by the geometric, spatial component of this pairing, and her left hemisphere is primarily involved in the algebraic, abstract concepts and processes involved.

This is a great way to make sure that your child learns in the most efficient way for her learning style and preferred intelligence. If your child is more spatial than analytical, or if she is more logical than creative, she does not have to be left out or penalized for her unique way of exercising her intelligence. Both sides of her brain are activated together, so her strong suit can support the weaker one.

Those familiar with Howard Gardner's theory of multiple intelligences know how important it is to approach learning with different intelligences in mind rather than depending solely on linguistic and logical-mathematical functions of the brain.[36]

Once again, these frequently activated connections between hemispheres of your child's brain create permanent pathways for adult problem solving, building the mathematical mind of which Maria Montessori spoke.[37]

---

[36] Gardner, Howard. *Frames of Mind: The Theory of Multiple Intelligences*. Basic Books, Inc.: New York. 1983.
[37] Montessori, *Psicoaritmetica*, p. 1.

3) Prefrontal Cortex

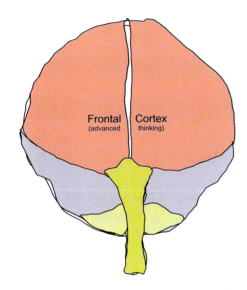

Because Montessori math materials promote active, discovery learning (see p. 38-39) and allow for self-monitoring and self-correction (see p. 41-42), they activate the prefrontal cortex, the most "advanced" part of your child's brain in terms of evolutionary development and higher powers of thinking.

If you want your child to use her brain to its fullest potential, you want her to exercise this higher part of her brain. Montessori math materials do this.

Getting the right answer to a problem can be quick and easy - and shallow; or it can be a little slower and more arduous - and produce a much deeper kind of learning. For example, I can tell your child that when she divides one fraction by another fraction, she can merely invert the second fraction and multiply. Or…I can show her how to use the fraction circles and allow her, through repeated experience and the recognition of patterns in those examples, to discover for herself how to generalize the rule for division of a fraction by a fraction.

The first approach draws heavily on the temporal lobe in your child's brain. The Montessori method of teaching fractions makes use of many more parts of her brain, most particularly that all-important prefrontal cortex.

The Montessori approach, rather than producing quick answers with little understanding behind them, creates a series of "Ah-ha!" moments of discovery. Your child's face lights up with delight at such moments, and these light bulb moments are centered in the frontal cortex.[38]

Jensen recognizes what Maria Montessori called the primacy of process over product. "Surprisingly, it doesn't matter to the brain whether it ever comes up with an answer. The neural growth happens because of the process, not the solution. A student could go to school for 12 years, rarely get right answers, and still have a well-developed brain."[39]

---

[38] Jensen. p. 92 and 96.
[39] Ibid. p. 36.

For success in later life - including higher math - there's just no contest between the two approaches as far as your child's brain goes. Montessori math grows your child's brain and produces an architecture of neural networks for higher thinking and problem solving that she will take with her into the rest of her life.

Conclusion

What we now know about the way your child's brain is designed, develops and functions leads us to conclude that the Montessori math materials will greatly assist her to properly grow and wire her brain as she goes about the task of learning mathematics.

Using multi-sensory, hands-on materials will foster the proliferation of neural connections among different lobes of her cerebellum. Using materials that provide geometric representations of algebraic generalizations will promote connections between the two hemispheres of her brain. And using materials that rely on self-correction and active, discovery learning will activate her pre-frontal cortex.

In short, using the Montessori math materials will create a more powerful brain in your child. They will allow her to hard-wire her brain for higher thinking, for creative problem-solving, and for logical processing of information.

When Maria Montessori created these materials to develop the child's "mathematical mind," she had no way of demonstrating that this meant a literal building of the internal structure of the child's brain. It is a tribute to her genius that she anticipated so many of the things we have learned since her death about the human brain.

Chapter 5
Montessori Math, Standards and Testing

I can still hear some parents asking anxiously, "But is my child where he is supposed to be in math with all these Montessori materials? And how will he do on that standardized test next spring?"

Every parent wants his or her child to be at or above "grade level" in mathematics, and it's hard to measure that with unfamiliar materials and teaching practices. In our test-driven society, those all-important test scores are viewed as the gold standard of success and accountability.

How does Montessori mathematics do in light of these questions?

State Standards

For many years, I can remember telling teachers in training that if they just follow the Montessori curriculum, their students will meet the requirements of state standards. I believed that, but I was also asking the teachers to believe without anything other than anecdotal evidence.

Several years ago, my wife and I decided to examine the Montessori curriculum against the state standards in Arizona. Many of our teacher trainees in Arizona were working in charter schools, and meeting state standards determined whether their schools continued to be funded.

What we found, specifically in the area of mathematics, is that the Montessori program actually exceeds Arizona standards in all but a few cases. We reached this conclusion after examining every one of the hundreds of performance objectives for students in grades 1-6 and aligning the Montessori curriculum with those objectives.

"Particular areas of performance objectives in which Montessori generally exceeds the state standards include number sense and operations, patterns and algebra, geometry and measurement, structure and logic. Areas outside the traditional Montessori Math curriculum include estimation, probability, and discrete mathematics, and objectives in those areas are met either with cultural curriculum lessons or with supplementary extensions of the Montessori curriculum."[40]

When I later compared Arizona standards with similar benchmarks from several other states, I reached the same conclusion. A small number of non-compliance items varied, depending on the specific curriculum of each state. But the core components were consistent - learning to add, subtract, multiply and divide with whole numbers in the early grades and then doing the same operations with fractions and decimals in the later grades. In these core areas, Montessori exceeded state standards in every case.

In Montessori, your child's ability to count whole numbers, fractions and decimals is always a year or two ahead of the state standards. Starting with the number rods in pre-primary classes, through the golden beads and bead chains, your child can count into the 1,000s while state standards are still calling for him to count to 100. His understanding of place value within the decimal system, based on the concrete experience of the golden bead materials, is certainly superior to what he can learn from numbers on a page in a textbook.

As for the four basic operations of addition, subtraction, multiplication and division, your child is introduced to multiplication and division when state standards call for just addition and subtraction. And he is using the golden beads and stamp game to calculate problems into four digits while standards call for only one- or two-digit problems.

The same edge appears later, when your child learns to do all of the operations with fractions of different denominators and with mixed numbers a year or two before expected by the standards.

---

[40] Duffy, Michael and D'Neil. *Meeting Arizona State Standards with the Montessori Curriculum.* Center for Montessori Teacher Education / New York: New York. 2004. p. 1.

Performance objectives in these areas far outnumber those in areas like estimation, reading charts and graphs, and set theory - which are not covered by the traditional Montessori curriculum. Montessori teachers simply need to fill in those few areas with a little creative use of the materials - called "extensions" in traditional Montessori circles - rather than abandon the Montessori curriculum for a textbook approach.

Standardized Tests

Standardized tests are not the best way to gauge the effectiveness of the teaching or learning process for your child, according to the consensus of education experts - despite the opinions of politicians and, perhaps, the perception of the general public.

W. James Popham, writing in the respected *Educational Leadership* magazine of the Association for Supervision and Curriculum Development, states that "a standardized test provides a misleading estimate of a school staff's effectiveness."[41]

Among the problems he cites with standardized testing is that these tests are designed to eliminate items most students can answer correctly and are limited, by time constraints, in the number of items they can present to demonstrate student competence. In sum, these tests don't deliver what most of us think they do.

A later issue of the same journal examines a variety of assessment techniques that are more effective means of promoting learning and accountability. The editor in chief, in an introduction to the issue, says that in contrast to standardized tests, such "formative assessment" blurs the line between instruction and assessment, involves students so that they care about learning and not just grades, provides meaningful feedback, and examines how students think.[42]

Whatever the opinions of the educational experts, standardized testing is here to stay for the foreseeable future, and all educators need to find a way to maximize the benefits and minimize the risks to student learning.

There are specific difficulties with standardized testing for your child because of the Montessori approach, particularly in light of the order and timing of the various elements of mathematics. These tests are totally geared to

---

[41] Popham, W. James. "Why Standardized Tests Don't Measure Educational Quality." *Educational Leadership*. The Association for Supervision and Curriculum Development: Alexandria, VA. Volume 56, Number 6, March 1999. p. 8.

whether he can get the right answer to a problem, with no attention to the level of understanding used to reach that answer - just the reverse of the emphasis in Montessori.

Furthermore, Montessori teaches understanding before memorization, but the standardized tests are designed to elicit quick answers from memory. At some stages of your child's progress in mathematics, his memorization skills may lag behind his understanding, producing temporary declines in his test scores.

All that having been said, your child should have no trouble holding his own on a standardized math test if he completes a Montessori three-year cycle of learning, has been given the full range of Montessori lessons and has been allowed to practice regularly with the materials.

In the 21 years that my wife and I ran a Montessori school in rural West Georgia, our students consistently scored well on standardized tests. Interestingly, we found that they tended to perform at about the national average in their first year of lower or upper elementary, mirroring the bell curve typical of the national norm. Then, most of them would blossom into the upper ranges in the third year of each three-year cycle.

As we worked with public and charter school Montessori programs over the years, these schools consistently placed in the top range of schools in their districts in test scores. There is certainly no scientific proof in these anecdotal observations, but it is reassuring to know that there is evidence to show that Montessori math education is producing good results on standardized tests.

---

[42] Scherer, Marge. "Reclaiming Testing." *Educational Leadership*. The Association for Supervision and Curriculum Development: Alexandria, VA. Volume 63, Number 3, November 2005, p. 9.

Teaching to the Test

Despite all the anecdotal evidence and the reassurances of veteran Montessori teachers, it's tempting to abandon the Montessori math materials and concentrate on getting students ready for the test the old-fashioned way - memorize and drill. Parents sometimes advocate vigorously for this approach, and Montessori schools and teachers sometimes agree to their demands.

I strongly suspect that this approach can produce marginally higher test scores in the short term for your child. It probably would take him less time to memorize his tables with flash cards than to use all the various tools available for memorization in a Montessori class. This gives a much faster access to the right answer than using materials like the strip boards, finger boards and snake games.

If I tell your child the "tricks" about inverting the second fraction in a division problem or counting the decimal places in the multiplicand and multiplier to figure out where to place the decimal point in the product, he will get the right answer a lot quicker than trying to figure out the "why" behind these tricks on his own through manipulation of the fraction materials or the decimal checkerboard.

However, I would argue that memorizing a "rule" someone else tells him produces less long-term learning and less understanding than arriving at the rule through his own discovery. Use of the Montessori materials actually should produce higher test scores over the long haul.

The bottom line for your child is that if his teacher abandons Montessori materials for textbook learning, his test score in next week's test might increase by a small margin. However, this is done at the price of losing all the psychological and developmental benefits we talked about in Chapter 3 and all the benefits for brain growth and development we talked about in Chapter 4.

That's too high a price for your child to pay for a few extra points on a test.

As Jensen puts it: "…if learning is what we value, then we ought to value the process of learning as much as the result of learning…Educators who insist on singular approaches and the 'right answer' are ignoring what's kept our species around for centuries…The notion of narrowed standardized tests to get the right answer violates the law of adaptiveness in a developing brain. Good quality education encourages the exploration of alternative thinking, multiple answers, and creative insights." [43]

 Teachers who trade quick, right answers for deeper understanding, long-term learning, developmentally healthy growth, and the building of your child's brain have betrayed you and your child for a few extra points on the test.

---

[43] Jensen. p. 16.

Chapter 6

A Plea to Parents

I would like to end this book with a series of pleas to you as parents of a Montessori student:

- Trust the benefits of Montessori mathematics and support the school, the teachers and your child.

- Don't try to help your child in mathematics by teaching her number tricks at home or doing a lot of drills.

- Don't pressure teachers to use workbooks or assign homework so you can have the satisfaction of seeing her progress.

- Don't judge your child's progress in mathematics only by standardized test scores or even her ability to get the right answers on your personal mini-tests.

- Learn more about Montessori mathematics and arrange some time to let your child show you what she has learned and how she does her work at school.

Trust and Support Montessori

Supportive parents understand the rationale behind the Montessori approach to education and its benefits for their child. Every parent wants the same thing for a child - to be healthy, happy and successful now and throughout her life. If you see Montessori education contributing to this goal, you will support the program.

That's not easy to do if you don't understand what we are doing or why we teach your child the way we do. The more you care about her welfare, the more likely you are to get nervous about her progress, particularly in the areas of reading and mathematics. The way we teach math is so foreign to your own experience that your doubts are understandable.

The purpose of this book is to resolve some of those doubts, clarifying the developmental benefits of the Montessori approach to mathematics for your child, making a case for the way Montessori math helps build her brain, and reassuring you about standards and tests.

If I was successful in those goals, perhaps you will come away from reading this book with a stronger belief in the Montessori approach to mathematics and more support for your school, the teachers, and in the final analysis, your child.

Your school needs your thoughtful questions and well-informed critique to make sure it is providing the very best education for your child. The better you understand the Montessori approach to education, the more this role of yours is healthy and helpful, and the more supportive you are likely to be.

Your child is the ultimate beneficiary of your understanding of the Montessori program. You will always be her primary educators, and she will be spared unnecessary confusion and operate at maximum efficiency if home and school operate out of a common vision.

Don't Try This at Home

While parental support is critically important for your child's success at school, I would urge you to avoid doing too much work with her at home in the area of mathematics. To reap the full benefits of Montessori math your child needs to work with the materials. You probably don't have golden beads, stamp games, bead frames, checkerboards or test tube division materials at home. Doing mathematics without the materials may only confuse your child or short-circuit the learning process if she is not yet ready for abstraction.

Please don't teach her those old tricks we learned to get the right answer. "Move the second partial product over one space in a two-digit multiplication problem…invert the divisor and multiply when you divide a fraction by a fraction…count the decimal places in the multiplier and multiplicand to know where to put the decimal in the product…etc."

Once your child knows an easy way to get the answer, there is little incentive for her to invest the time and effort to work with materials so she can understand where that answer comes from and what it means. With that, she loses all the developmental gains outlined in Chapter 3 and all the potential brain growth explained in Chapter 4. That's too high a price to pay for getting an easy answer!

Our society has a tendency to judge everything by the bottom line: Is the answer right? And how quickly did you get to the answer? Montessori is going against the grain in its approach to mathematics (and education in general). If you chose Montessori for your child, then you need to be willing to go against the grain yourself and support your child's Montessori way of learning.

Give up Your Need for Workbooks and Homework

You sometimes need to see your child's work to really believe. If only she would bring home some finished workbook pages in mathematics or some math problems to solve for homework so you could monitor her progress!

Resist the urge to pressure her teacher in this direction. You might satisfy your need, but it would be at the price of the teacher compromising on the Montessori program. That, in turn, could compromise developmental and brain growth benefits that come from working with the materials.

The more time your child spends at school filling out answers on a workbook page, the less time she will have to work with the Montessori materials. The more mathematics she is required to do, particularly of the rote drill variety, the less interesting math will be to her. The more skilled she gets at getting quick answers, the less incentive she has to deepen her understanding - or expand her brain power.

Homework has the added disadvantage of making it impossible for your child to use the materials to do the work, even if she were so inclined. If she puts in a full day's work at school, she shouldn't need to do any math homework - or any significant homework in any other subjects.

You might object that your child needs to get used to the idea of homework so she will be ready to move on to the next level of education in a traditional school. An independent, self-assured student who finds herself in a new situation will have no trouble figuring out what is expected of her. And why impose the drudgery of make-work assignments and mindless homework on your child one day before it's necessary![44]

Don't Evaluate the Program by Test Scores Alone

Test scores have an exaggerated place in our society today, and you quite naturally expect your child to have respectable scores on those standardized math tests.

However, I would urge you not to judge the whole program by those test scores. Even in a traditional school setting, test scores are only one, very limited and very imperfect tool for judging the success of a program.

Very talented and smart students sometimes do poorly on tests because of test phobia or anxiety, undermined by their own conscientious nature and drive for perfection or desire to please. This danger is greater in the current atmosphere of test mania and the accompanying high stakes feel of the whole testing experience.

In a Montessori context, those tests have the further disadvantage that they are not designed to measure the way we teach mathematics or what we value most for your child. The way we teach math starts with the process and ends up with memorization to make calculations faster and easier. The tests assume that he memorized first and should be able to apply that memory to simple problems.

Even more importantly, the tests don't measure what we value. They count and grade the number of correct answers, but they say nothing about the depth of your child's understanding of the path to those answers. They cannot measure the psychological development she has experienced. They cannot measure the growth of her brain.

---

[44] For a full discussion of the homework issue, see *The Homework Myth: Why Our Kids Get Too Much of a Bad Thing*, by Alfie Kohn. Da Capo Press, Philedphia, 2006.

Your child's teacher has other tools to assess how well your child is doing in mathematics and how much progress she is making. A good Montessori teacher learns more about her progress from daily observations of her work than from the once-a-year standardized tests. She is better able to evaluate your child's progress from watching her use the materials than from administering tests of her own.

Tests only tell us if she got a certain number of right answers. A teacher's observation of her level of understanding is a better indicator of whether she is developing psychologically and whether her brain is growing.

At home, subjecting your child to a parent-administered mini-test in math is no more valid in measuring those important outcomes than the school test. If your child is using materials and hasn't yet memorized her math facts, you will only undermine her confidence in herself by putting her on the spot with a pop quiz.

Rather than giving a math quiz, pay attention to your child's overall development. Is she more independent, self-assured, confident, emotionally secure, happy, relaxed, pleased with herself, and eager to go to school?

You, her parents, know her better than anyone else and can read these signs if you're paying attention to them. If you answer, "yes," to all or most of those questions, then you can probably be assured that she is making good progress in math - without a pop quiz.

Learn More About Montessori

Reading this book is a good indication that you want to know what your child is experiencing in this Montessori math program of hers. Don't stop there. Try to learn more - from parent education opportunities, from classroom observations, from open houses, and from talking to her about her work and use of the materials.

If there is a parent education night at your school, make sure you attend. Teachers spend a lot of time preparing to tell you what your child is doing in school, and this provides a unique opportunity for you to get it straight from the source most directly related to your child's math education.

If your school allows or encourages you to sit in the classroom as an observer, give it some priority and make time for it in your schedule. There's no book or theoretical explanation that can do as much as a few hours of watching real students - not just your own child - at work in a Montessori classroom.

If your school has an open house, where students demonstrate their work for their parents, make sure you attend with your child and ask her to show you how she does some of her work in the area of mathematics.

Talk to her about her math. You learned the names of some of the materials and their use in this book. Use it to engage in a conversation with your child and let her fill you in on the details.

And don't just stop at math. You can educate yourself about the whole Montessori program to be a more supportive parent.

Read books by Maria Montessori and about Montessori (your school should have a lending library of books for parents, or at least a recommended reading list). Go to every parent education program offered by your school - and don't be afraid to ask questions. Engage your child's teachers in conversation about Montessori practice through pre-arranged phone calls or scheduled conferences. Observe in your child's classroom several times a year, or try to schedule an observation at the next level if she is getting ready to move up a level in a year or two.

The more you know, the more you can support your child's development and growth. There's not a lot more important than that for a parent!

Appendix

Description and Use of Montessori Math Materials

Materials	Description	Use
	Numeration	
Number Rods	Ten wooden rods, from 10 cm to one meter, divided into units of alternating colors of red and blue.	To teach children to recognize quantities from 1-10.
Sandpaper Numerals	The numbers 0-9, in rough sandpaper, on smooth green boards.	To teach the numerals 0-9 and prepare the child for writing numbers.
Spindle Box	45 loose spindles and a box with compartments numbered from 0-9.	To teach children the concept of zero and matching quantities to number symbols from 0-9.
Numerals and Counters	Small red discs and cut-out numerals from 0-9.	To teach children to count from 1-10 and to introduce them, to the concept of odd and even numbers.
Golden Bead Introduction	One unit bead, a bar of 10 beads, a square of 100 beads, and a cube of 1000 beads, in a wooden tray.	Introduction to the decimal system.
Teen Boards	Two slotted boards with 10s in each space, wooden numbers from 1-9 to compose the numbers 11-19, with colored bead bars for 1-9.	To teach children to compose numbers from 11-19, matching number symbols to quantities in beads.
Tens Boards	Two slotted boards with the numbers 10-90, wooden numbers from 1-9, with bead bars.	To teach children to compose numbers from 10-99, matching number symbols to quantities in beads.

Hundred Board	Board with 100 squares, and wooden tiles with the numbers 1-100.	To teach children to count to 100 and know how to sequence the numbers 1-100.
Bead Cabinet	Chains of beads in multiples of 1-10, with short versions to the square of each number and long chains to the cubes, squares and cubes of 1-10.	To teach children to count to 1000, with skip counting numbered arrows to mark the end of each multiple of 1-10.
Geometric Hierarchy	Scale sized and color coded unit cube (cm^3), ten prism, hundred square, thousand cube, ten thousand prism, hundred thousand square, and million cube.	To introduce children to the relative size of hierarchies from units to millions.
Fraction Circles	Green metal squares with red circles from a whole to divided parts representing halves to tenths.	To teach children how to recognize fractional numbers and quantities from halves to tenths.
Decimal Fraction Materials	Yellow board with columns for units to millions and tenths to millionths, with color-coded cubes (or discs) to represent the decimal numbers.	To teach children how to create decimal numbers in hierarchies from tenths to millionths.

Operations

Golden Bead Materials	Unit beads, bars of 10 beads, squares of 100 beads and cubes of 1000 beads.	To teach childen the process of addition, subtraction, multiplication, and division in the most concrete way, with problems up to four digits.
Number Cards	Large and small number card sets with units 1-9, tens 10-90, hundreds 100-900, and thousands 1000-9000.	Used with the golden bead materials for construction of number symbols up to 9999 and recording of calculations for four operations.
Dot Board	White board with a grid of small squares in which to put dots with a water-based pen, with columns of squares from units to 10,000s.	Allows children to practice decimal system addition with many addends, and answers that go into five digits.
Stamp Game	Green (units), blue (tens), red (100s), and green (1000s) wooden "stamps" with similarly colored skittles and markers.	To teach children the four operations up to four digits with a material one step toward abstraction from the golden beads (symbolic quantities).

Small Bead Frame	Abacus-like frame of beads on wires, with green beads to represent units, blue for tens, red for hundreds and green again for 1000s.	To teach children addtion, subtraction and multiplication, with answers into five digits, in a step toward full abstraction.
Large Bead Frame	Abacus-like frame of beads on wires, with the green-blue-red pattern for simple numbers and for thousands, and one line of green beads for units of millions.	To teach children compound multilication, with multi-digit multipliers and answers into the millions (uses notation to move toward abstraction).
Checkerboard	A checkerboard pattern of green, blue, and red squares representing hierarchies up to 100,000,000,000, with colored bead bars and number tiles.	To allow practice of compound multiplication with four-digit multipliers and nine-digit multiplicands, in steps leading to full abstraction.
Flat Bead Frame	Abacus-style frame of beads with all beads in gold and wires up to the hierarchy of 100,000.	To bring children to full abstraction in compound multiplication problems.
Bank Game	Set of number cards from 1-9 to 1,000,000-9,000,000, with mulpliers cards in green, blue and red to 9999.	To allow a group of children to practice compound multiplication in a cooperative game.
Racks and Tubes	Test tubes filled with color-coded beads representing hierarchies up to 1,000,000, with four color-coded boards on which to distribute the dividend.	To teach children to do long division problems with divisors up to four digits and dividends into the millions, moving toward full abstraction.
Fraction Circles	Box containing whole circles, halves, thirds, fourths, fifths, sixths, sevenths, eighths, ninths and tenths. Four fraction skittles for division.	To teach children how to add, subtract, multiply and divide proper and improper fractions, in a process that allows them to discover the rules themselves.
Centesimal Frame	A black metal square, with a circle divided into 100 even arcs to fit and measure fraction circle pieces.	To allow children to translate fraction pieces into equivalent decimals and / or percents.
Decimal Fraction Board	Yellow board with columns for units to millions and tenths to millionths, with color-coded cubes (or discs) to represent the decimal numbers.	To teach children how to add, subtract, multiply and divide decimal fractions.
Decimal Checkerboard	Square checkerboard with green, blue, and red pattern to represent whole numbers and lighter colored green, blue and red pattern to represent decimals.	To teach children how to multiply decimals in such a way that they discover for themselves the rules for the placement of the decimal point in the product.

Peg Board	A framed square of peg board, with green, blue, and red pegs and colored cups to hold te pegs.	To research LCM and GCF; to create squares of binomial and trinomial numbers; to guide the extraction of square roots of numbers into 100,000s.
Cubing Materials	One cube and 27 squares for each number from 1-9, color-coded to match the bead bar colors.	To allow children to construct cubes of binomials and trinomials, with arithematical values.
Binomial and Trinomial Cubes	Cubes composed of nine and 27 parts respectively, in red, blue, yellows and black colors, with cubes and prisms combined to form the full cube.	To represent the algebric formula, n geometric form, of binomial and trinomial cubes. The dimensions of the parts give the terms of the formula.
Hierarchical Trinomial Cube	Cube with the same parts as the trinomial cube, but with colors changed to match the hierarchical value of each piece (red, yellow, orange, brown, blue, white).	To guide the extraction of the cube root of a seven- to nine-digit number.

Memorization

Addition Strip Board	Board with the numbers 1-18 across the top and a grid on which to place the strips - sets of blue and red strips to each represent the numbers 1-9.	To help children memorize the addition combinations or "facts" of the addition tables.
Addition Working Charts	Two control charts of all the addition facts, four working boards with all 100 answers to a blank board, and box of addition equations and sums.	To help children memorize the addition combinations or "facts" of the addition tables.
Addition Snake Game	A black and white bead stair of 1-9, colored bead bars to represent the numbers 1-9, and a box of ten bars.	To help children memorize the addition combinations or "facts" of the addition tables, using a game of changing a colored snake to gold.
Subtraction Strip Board	Board with the numbers 1-18 across the top and a grid on which to place the strips - sets of blue, red, and neutral strips.	To help children memorize the subtraction combinations or "facts" of the subtraction tables.

Subtraction Working Charts	A control charts of all the subtraction facts, two working boards with all answers and a blank board, and box of subtraction equations and sums.	To help children memorize the subtraction combinations or "facts" of the subtraction tables.
Negative Snake Game	A black and white bead stair of 1-9, a red and white bead stair of 1-9, colored bead bars to represent positive numbers, and grey bead bars for negative numbers.	To help children memorize the subtraction combinations or "facts" of the subtraction tables, by changing a colored snake to gold and grey.
Multiplication Board	A square board with indentations for 100 red beads, with 1-10 across the top for the multiplier and a slot for the mulplicand on the side.	To help children memorize the multiplication combinations or "facts" of the multiplication tables.
Multiplication Working Charts	Two control charts of all the multiplication facts, three working boards with all 100 answers to a blank board, and box of multiplication equations and products.	To help children memorize the multiplication combinations or "facts" of the multiplication tables.
Decanomial Bead Bars	Color-coded bead bars from 1-10, with enough in each compartment to construct the geometric decanomial square.	To help children memorize the multiplication combinations or "facts" of the multiplication tables, recognizing the pattern formed by the combinations.
Table of Pythagoras	Colored-coded squares and rctangles to allow construction of the decanomial square.	To help children memorize the multiplication combinations or "facts" of the multiplication tables, recognizing the pattern formed by the combinations.
Division Board	A square board with indentations for 100 green beads, with placement holes for skittles for 1-10 across the top for the divisor.	To help children memorize the division combinations or "facts" of the division tables.
Division Working Charts	A control chart of all the division facts, and two working charts, one with all the quotients and the other blank, with box of division equations and quotients.	To help children memorize the division combinations or "facts" of the division tables.

Bibliography

Duffy, Michael and D'Neil. *Children of the Universe: Cosmic Education in the Montessori Elementary Classroom*, Parent Child Press: Hollidaysburg, PA, 2002.

Duffy, Michael and D'Neil. *Meeting Arizona State Standards with the Montessori Curriculum*. Center for Montessori Teacher Education / New York: New York. 2004.

Gardner, Howard. *Frames of Mind: The Theory of Multiple Intelligences*. Basic Books, Inc.: New York. 1983.

Howard, Pierce J. *The Owner's Manual for the Brain: Everyday Applications from Mind-Brain Research*. Bard Press: Austin, TX, 2000.

Jensen, Eric. *Teaching with the Brain in Mind*. Association for Supervision and Curriculum Development: Alexandria, VA, 1998.

Kohn, Alfie. *The Homework Myth: Why Our Kids Get Too Much of a Bad Thing*, Da Capo Press: Philadelphia, 2006.

Lillard, Angeline Stoll. *Montessori: The Science Behind the Genius*, New York: Oxford University Press, 2005.

Montessori, Maria. *The Absorbent Mind*. Dell Publishing: New York. 1984.

Montessori, Maria. *Psicoaritmetica: L'aritmetica sviluppata secondo le indicazioni della psicologia infantile durante venticinque anni di esperienze..* Garzanti, 1971.

Montessori, Maria. *The Secret of Childhood*. Fides Publishers: Notre Dame, Indiana. 1966.

Popham, W. James. "Why Standardized Tests Don't Measure Educational Quality." *Educational Leadership.* The Association for Supervision and Curriculum Development: Alexandria, VA. Volume 56, Number 6, March 1999.

Scherer, Marge. "Reclaiming Testing." *Educational Leadership*. The Association for Supervision and Curriculum Development: Alexandria, VA. Volume 63, Number 3, November 2005.

Stigler, J.W. (1984) "Mental Abacus: The effect of abacus training on Chinese children's mental calculation." *Educational Psychologist*, 35 (2)

Sylwester, Robert. *A Biological Brain in a Cultural Classroom: Enhancing Cognitive and Social Development Through Collaborative Classroom Management*. Corwin Press Inc.: Thousand Oaks, CA. 2nd Edition. 2003.

Wolf, Aline. *Nurturing the Spirit in Non-Sectarian Classrooms*, Parent Child Press: Hollidaysburg, PA, 1996.

Zull, James E. *The Art of Changing the Brain: Enriching the Practice of Teaching by Exploring the Biology of Learning*. Stylus Publishing: Sterling, VA. 2002

About the Author

Michael Duffy has been a Montessori classroom teacher and a teacher-trainer for the Center for Montessori Teacher Education / New York for almost 20 years. This experience has given him a passion for the beauty and effectiveness of the Montessori math materials.

Michael holds American Montessori Society credentials at the 6-12 age level and taught both lower and upper elementary classes at the Blackstock Montessori School in Villa Rica, GA, a school founded and operated for 21 years by his wife, D'Neil. He also holds a masters degree in education, with a specialty in media education.

As a teacher-trainer, he has taught adults in New York, Toronto, Phoenix, AZ, Lexington, MA, Vancouver and Puerto Rico. The teacher-trainees in these programs are spread throughout North America, and Michael has visited some 100 classrooms in 20 states, in three provinces of Canada and in Puerto Rico.

He has also served as a private Montessori consultant for schools, guiding curriculum development, setting up school libraries, and giving parent education and in-service training sessions for teachers. And he has given keynote presentations and workshops at national and international Montessori and non-Montessori conferences.

He has written articles for Montessori Life and co-authored with his wife the book *Children of the Universe: Cosmic Education in the Montessori Elementary Classroom*.

The part of this book related to brain research comes from his long interest in the field, from professional workshops and seminars, and from a selection of recently published books.

Michael and his wife currently live in the Shenandoah Valley of Virginia. They have two adult children and four grandchildren.